SELF-DE

—WI

I CHING

A New Interpretation

Dedicated to the memory of my much respected father, James Sneddon, whose wisdom and advice have sustained me in all my endeavours, and to my mother Isabel from whom I inherited compassion for my fellow human beings. My thanks also go to my wife, Carol, and daughter, Jacqueline, whose presence have enriched my life and served to remind me of the human, caring nature of the *I Ching*.

SELF-DEVELOPMENT
— WITH THE —
I CHING
A New Interpretation

— Paul Sneddon —

foulsham
LONDON • NEW YORK • TORONTO • SYDNEY

foulsham

Yeovil Road, Slough, Berkshire SL1 4JH

ISBN 0-572-01529-1

Printed in Great Britain by Cox & Wyman Ltd, Reading, Berkshire

CONTENTS

INTRODUCTION

The *I Ching* is the ancient Chinese book of wisdom and divination, known as the *Book of Changes*. For thousands of years, it has been used by the Chinese as an oracle — something to consult when knowledge of the future is sought. As such, although it would appear initially to fit into the category of fortune-telling, along with tarot cards, palmistry and astrology, it is far older than any of these. Furthermore, its readings are often uncannily accurate, and this explains the reason it has been called the ultimate oracle.

It has been said that the *I Ching* owes its success to the fact that its pronouncements are almost entirely composed of platitudes, mostly vague, and that it is easy to read any interpretation into their amorphous content. At first sight, this may appear to be the case. The situation is further complicated by the flowery language and obscure terminology of the text, although it must be remembered that the *I Ching* was written thousands of years ago, in the language of the day. In the same way, the pronouncements were formed within the framework of events prevailing at that time. Thus, many of the original pronouncements relate to the antiquated symbolism of battles, feudal princes and foreign animals. Phrases indicating good or bad auspices and success or failure were used to assist the practice of divination.

In the thousands of years since the book was written, many eminent scholars have translated it from Chinese into Latin, German, English, and a host of other languages. In recent years, several attempts have been made to render it into modern-day language, but none have succeeded in being able to retain the depth of meaning that the *I Ching* contains. The reader has therefore been faced either with having to flounder in a sea of obscure language, in the case of earlier versions, or with having to accept the more incomplete meanings of later versions.

In the last few decades, interest in the *I Ching* has spread to the West, and the book has many adherents who treat its judgements with suprising seriousness. It is therefore regrettable that the amorphous nature of the book's text tends to disallow a much greater following. With this is mind, I set myself the task of simplifying the book, by translating it into modern-day language and terminology.

Assisted by the copious notes of previous scholars, I carefully removed all the old symbolism and reference to battles, princes and foreign animals, without detracting in any way from the context of the original. In doing so, I took great care not to fall into the trap of translating the book into modern-day language only to make its relevance solely applicable to the present day.

This version of the *I Ching*, which I refer to as the *New I Ching*, removes entirely the vagueness of the original readings whilst retaining in its entirety the meaning of the text. The answers obtained by using the *New I Ching* will be much more to the point and it is hoped that this new version will encourage the use of the book by many more people.

THE ORIGINAL *I CHING*

THE CONCEPT OF CHANGE

The *I Ching* or *Book of Changes* is aptly named: it is a book that charts the changes that occur continuously in life. To understand what the ancient authors meant by change, one has to gain some insight into Eastern thought. The human brain is split into two hemispheres, left and right, separated by a large nerve track called the *corpus callosum*. Whereas we in the West mostly use the left hemisphere, the 'reality-testing' side, people born in the Eastern world use the right hemisphere, the 'imagination' side. We are all born with the same kind of brain. It is our upbringing that determines the side we use. In the West, children initially use the 'imagination' side of the brain, but we are taught as we grow older to suppress the imagination in favour of more rational, logical thought. In the East this does not happen to the same extent.

This is best illustrated in the differing approaches of East and West to problems. Whereas in the West we tend to approach them in a straightforward logical manner, the Eastern approach is more imaginative, and indirect.

In a contest, the Westerner will attempt to win by considering how best victory may be achieved in the shortest possible time. In contrast, the Easterner will strive to anticipate the actions of the opponent, in order both to thwart such actions and also to turn them to personal advantage. The recent growth in popularity in the West of Eastern martial arts, provides us with an example. In a fight, the Westerner will consider only how to bring an opponent to the ground in the quickest fashion and will be the first to 'strike out'. The Easterner will await and anticipate the blow and will attempt to use the opponent's own actions against them, by moving with, rather than against, the impetus of the blow.

The belief that it is more sensible to move *with* the forces of nature rather than against them, is a very sound attitude. For thousands of years, the Chinese have symbolised the opposing forces of nature as Yin and Yang. Even today, many ailments are attributed to either an excess or deficit of Yin or Yang in the body.

Originally, Yin symbolised shade, Yang, light, and the concept of opposites was thus indicated. Yin was used to describe the female or passive elements, Yang, the male, or active. In Western terms, Yin is negative, Yang, positive. Many Chinese believe that life and nature consist of a flow between Yin and Yang and that everything is constantly changing. As the seasons occur and reoccur, so does life consist successively of cycles of destruction and reconstruction.

The *I Ching* teaches how the 'Chuntzu,' or 'Superior Man,' should behave. It states that the proper and good life is achieved by the Chuntzu when his life is in harmony with the flux of Yin and Yang and when he moves with the continuous advance and regression of the vital forces of nature. In this way will he move towards an expanding awareness and universal spirit.

To be in harmony with the flow of nature, one must also be reconciled to the concept of cyclic change. In the West, we fight change whenever and wherever it occurs, believing basically that change is bad. Even change that is obviously for the better, we view with suspicion and dislike.

Change, however, is inevitable. Cyclic change is even more so. Nature is built upon cyclic change: as winter follows summer, as night follows day, so occur the changes in every aspect of life. Things cannot continually improve, neither can they continually decay. There has of necessity to be an end somewhere, a breathing space. At that point, reversal sets in and the process begins anew. So it is with life itself. Birth is without exception followed by death. Good is followed by bad; bad by good. History shows that peace is always followed by war; war by peace. Permissiveness is followed by puritanism; puritanism by permissiveness. Fashions die out, only to reappear later.

Only by accepting the inevitability of, and by conforming to, cyclic change, can harmony be achieved and peace of mind attained. It is this basic tenet that embodies the concept of change in the *I Ching*.

HISTORY OF THE *I CHING*

In essence, the *I Ching* is a collection of 64 short essays based on ancient Chinese philosophy. A question is asked and the manipulation of sticks or coins results in the random selection of one of the essays, which is then supposed to relate in some way to the question. The essays are represented by 64 symbolic figures known as 'hexagrams'. These are figures composed of six broken or solid lines. It is more correct to state that each hexagram is composed of two 'trigrams', each of which in turn comprises three broken or solid lines. It is interesting that some two thousand years elapsed between the devising of the trigrams and the devising of the hexagrams.

In 3322 BC, the Emperor Fu-hsi sought to differentiate between the two opposing forces of nature, Yin and Yang. He chose a broken line (— —) to represent Yin, and a solid line (———) to represent Yang. Whether by whimsy or by reasoning all of his own, he created four new figures by creating combinations of broken and solid lines (⚎, ⚏, ⚌ and ⚍). His next step was to create the trigrams, by the process of adding either a broken or a solid line to each of these four figures. In this way were the eight trigrams formed. He gave a name to each of them, the names representing their natural attributes and symbols. The trigrams and their meanings are shown in Figure 1 on page 11.

It is easy to see how the ancient authors linked the attributes to the images and symbols. For instance, a mountain is obviously an obstacle, something that arrests progress. The flames of a fire are bright and beautiful. In thunder there is a great element of movement and perilousness. Similar connections can be seen between the other attributes, images and symbols. The male attributes indicate power and movement, the female attributes, pleasure and passivity.

These trigrams have been called the most ancient utterances of the mind of man. Possibly they are. Suffice it to say that they were in use five thousand years ago. Tortoiseshells have been unearthed, dating back to that period, on which are inscribed the eight trigrams. There is some evidence to suggest that the trigrams were used as an early aid to divination.

FIGURE 1 — THE EIGHT TRIGRAMS

Trigram	*Name*	*Attributes, images and symbols*		
☰	Ch'ien	creative, male, active	heaven	father
☷	K'un	receptive, female, passive	earth	mother
☳	Chen	movement, perilousness	thunder	1st son
☵	K'an	pit, danger	water	2nd son
☶	Ken	arresting progress	mountain	3rd son
☴	Sun	gentle penetration	wood, wind	1st daughter
☲	Li	brightness, beauty	fire	2nd daughter
☱	Tui	pleased satisfaction	marsh, lake	3rd daughter

Figure 1. The eight trigrams with their names and attributes

Over the next two thousand years, the Chinese developed their remarkable early culture. In the year 2850 BC, the legendary Golden Age of China began. The likewise legendary Hsia dynasty commenced in 2205 BC, to be followed by the Shang dynasty in

1600 BC, which in turn lasted until the advent of the Chou dynasty in 1027 BC. It was in the closing years of the Shang dynasty that the hexagrams were formed and devised, by the founder of the Chou dynasty, King Wen.

In the year 1143 BC he was imprisoned by the emperor in Yu-li, in the province of Ho-nan. It was in this and the following year that he devised the hexagrams by the process of forming the eight trigrams into all of the permutations that could be made by the joining of any two trigrams. The result was the 64 hexagrams, as illustrated in Figure 2 on page 13–15.

Several of the hexagrams appear to have the same Chinese names. This is owing to the subtle peculiarities of the Chinese language. It will be seen from the English equivalents of the names, however, that the actual meanings are completely different. King Wen interpreted the meanings of the hexagrams and composed 64 short essays to accompany them. These are what constitute the prophecies; they are called the 'Judgements'. An interesting fact is that the hexagrams and their Judgements alone, form the *I Ching* proper. Everything else is by nature commentary or explanation of the text of the Judgements. All that King Wen did was to devise the hexagrams and interpret them in his Judgements.

Some time in the next sixty years, at least no later than his death in 1105 BC, King Wen's son, the Duke of Chou, composed the lines. These were his interpretations of the meanings of the individual broken or solid lines, within the context of each hexagram. He interpreted the meanings of all 384 lines, keeping within the general meanings of the hexagrams as interpreted by his father. In this way, he carried on his father's work, by expanding the divinatory capabilities of the hexagrams.

For the next 600 years, the Chinese began to use the *I Ching* as an oracle and an aid to divination. Confucius himself was greatly influenced by the book and much of what we know today as Confucianism is based on it, as is much of Taoism. Towards the end of his life, Confucius decided to add his own comments to the book. In 483 BC, he wrote his celebrated 'Commentaries' and 'Symbolisms' to the *I Ching*. The Commentaries are his remarks on the Judgements of King Wen; the Symbolisms, his remarks on the Lines of the Duke of Chou.

Throughout the centuries, thousands of scholars have tried to the best of their abilities to interpret the *I Ching*. They were not assisted by the complexities of the Chinese language. One of the

FIGURE 2 — THE 64 HEXAGRAMS.

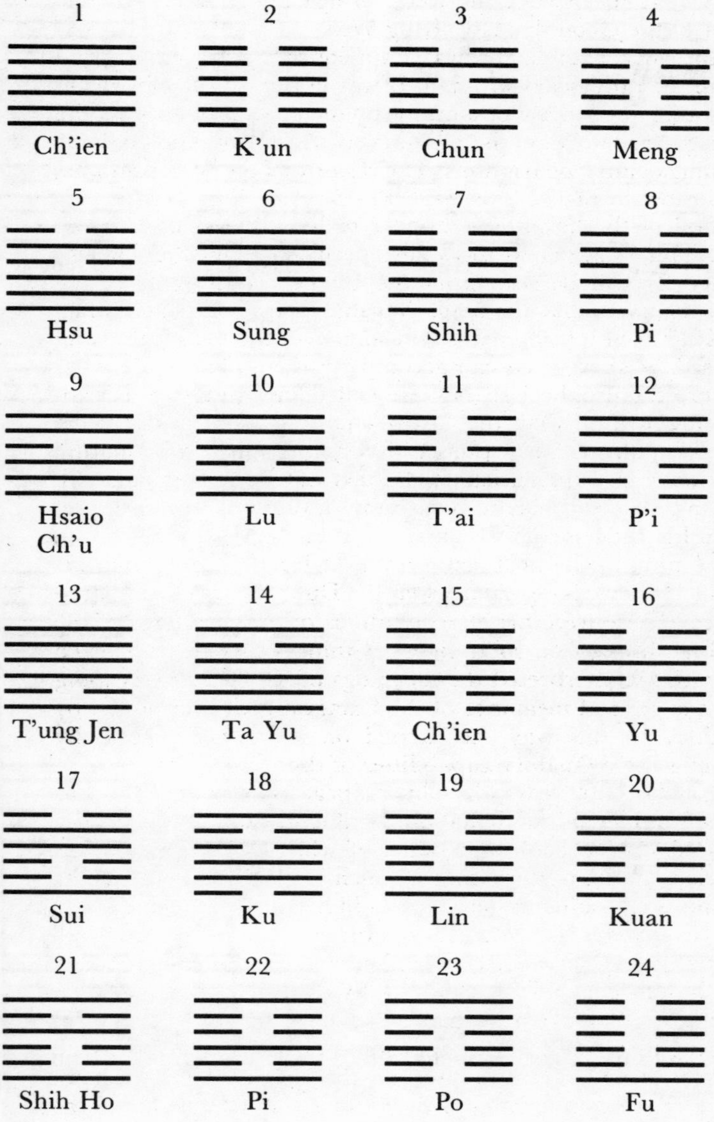

1	2	3	4
Ch'ien	K'un	Chun	Meng
5	6	7	8
Hsu	Sung	Shih	Pi
9	10	11	12
Hsaio Ch'u	Lu	T'ai	P'i
13	14	15	16
T'ung Jen	Ta Yu	Ch'ien	Yu
17	18	19	20
Sui	Ku	Lin	Kuan
21	22	23	24
Shih Ho	Pi	Po	Fu

25	26	27	28
Wu Wang	Ta Ch'u	I	Ta Kuo
29	30	31	32
K'an	Li	Hsien	Heng
33	34	35	36
Tun	Ta Chuang	Chin	Ming I
37	38	39	40
Chia Jen	K'uei	Chien	Chieh
41	42	43	44
Sun	I	Kuai	Kou
45	46	47	48
Ts'ui	Sheng	K'un	Ching

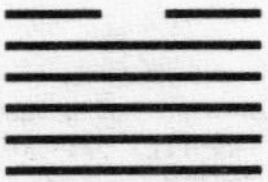

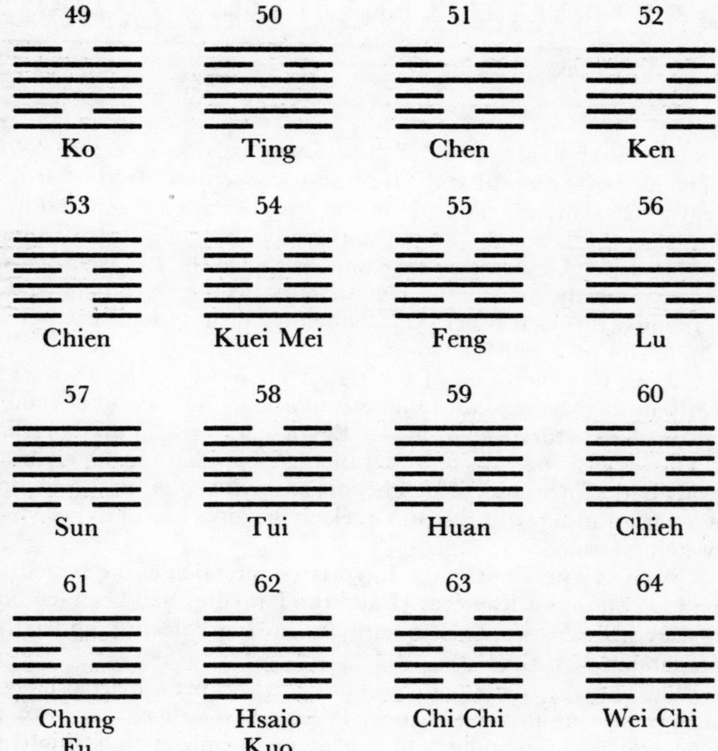

Figure 2. The 64 hexagrams and their Chinese names

most significant contributors to the translation of the book was Richard Wilhelm; another was the nineteenth century Sinologist, James Legge. The latter's approach was different to that of his predecessors in that, whereas earlier translators had mainly translated verbatim from the Chinese, Legge realised that the individual characters in the Chinese language were not so much words, rather they were expressions of complete ideas or concepts. So it was that he was able to render the *I Ching* into the classic version as it stands today wherein the readings closely approximate the original ideas of the authors at the time of their writing.

RELIGION AND THE *I CHING*

To understand the nature of the *I Ching*, it is necessary to have some idea of the world at the time of its conception. In the twelfth century BC, Chinese life had for centuries been of a feudal nature. Rival warlords fought amongst themselves, each commanding the loyalties of their subjects. China was even then an isolationist society, mostly due to the fact that its people were constantly warring with each other. Consequently, little influence entered China from the outside world.

China was then one of the oldest civilisations in the world. Only in the Mediterranean area could be found any other semblance of structured civilisation. Egypt had been flourishing for centuries and was now on the wane. Minoan and Hittite civilisations had grown and died. Phoenician civilisation was growing, and was trading with Egypt. Greek civilisation was in the process of being formed.

A century previously, the Egyptian oppression of the Israelites had begun under Rameses II and the Israelites had been led out of Egypt by Moses, subsequently to invade Palestine under the leadership of Joshua.

The worship of many different deities was prevalent, although it may be true to say that only in Egypt was there any form of state-organised religion and it can be surmised that this was brought about by the Pharaohs solely as a measure of self-preservation. A far older religion existed and was practised by the Israelites. It was the world's first great monotheist religion, Judaism. Although Judaism in its basic form had been practised by the Jews since the birth of their race, it only took an organised and positive form when Moses led the Jewish tribes out of Egypt and presented them with the Ten Commandments.

This was in approximately 1230 BC, 87 years before King Wen devised the hexagrams and wrote his Judgements. Whether there was any connection between the imposition of the law of Moses and the composition of the *I Ching* is a matter for conjecture. The two civilisations were, for various reasons, unlikely to have had any intercourse. There is no evidence to show that the two peoples were even aware of each other's existence. The Jews were busy building a new home for themselves and the Chinese were engaged in the battles that attended the death of one dynasty and the birth of another. Added to this, Judaism could never be described as a proselytising religion. To be a Jew is to have been born one. It is therefore unlikely that the Jews would have attempted to spread the beliefs and codes of behaviour to which they subscribed.

Having said that, the fact remains that basic tenets of the Ten Commandments are uncannily similar to the Judgements in the *I Ching*. In the former, the Jews were told that they should not kill, commit adultery, bear false witness, commit idolatry, steal or covet their neighbours' wives or goods — sensible stipulations for the formulation of a structured society. By comparison, the Judgements of the *I Ching* are full of many similar admonitions to behave in a socially acceptable way.

How then did the Judgements of King Wen and the Lines of his son, the Duke of Chou, so closely resemble the code of behaviour imposed by Moses on the Jews? Perhaps there existed at that time a universal belief in the difference between right and wrong, but that is rather doubtful. Certainly, the Judgements and Lines resembled little more than a collection of omens, such as the belief that black cats are unlucky. Every society develops these and they could be expected to be especially popular in a warring society. Omen tablets have been discovered which date back to Babylonian culture in 2000 BC, and it is possible that some Babylonian omens could have found their way into Chinese life. The Babylonians, however, were not renowned for their good behaviour and so it is unlikely that their omens had any influence on the formation of the *I Ching*.

There is some evidence to suggest that the Chinese themselves had developed their society along the lines of propriety and correct behaviour. This is possible, when one considers that their society encouraged politeness towards each other, rather than to any religious dictates. It is also conceivable that a society such as that of the Chinese, could have developed a collective 'greenhouse' mentality, not doing unto others, in case they do it to you. This would contain the necessary binding ingredient — fear. Whereas religious devotees would usually stop themselves from performing certain deeds, for fear of divine retribution in the next world, the possessor of a greenhouse mentality would similarly desist from wrong-doing for fear of human retribution in this world.

The Chinese had long believed in the mystical properties of nature. They observed cyclic change in the passing of the seasons and applied this to human behaviour. They firmly believed also in the oneness of the universe. Everything was intimately interconnected. If a person were to move an arm to the right, it was their belief that the entire universe would move with it. From this came their belief in the common good. Good behaviour towards one person had the effect of adding to the good of society as a whole. A parallel can be drawn with the words spoken by Christ a thousand years later when He said that whatsoever was done for the least of His brethren was done also for him.

Another significant fact is the relationship between Buddhism and the writing by Confucius of his Commentaries and Symbolisms to the *I Ching*. As far as can be seen, there is no apparent relationship between the two and certainly no evidence to indicate that the two cultures from which the two men came ever had any intercourse. Nevertheless, the two men were certainly contemporaries. The Buddha died in 480 BC; Confucius died the year after, 479 BC. This is a significant coincidence.

So, we are still none the wiser. Was the compilation of the *I Ching* affected by outside influences, or was it purely the product of Chinese philosophy at that time? The believer in a god, regardless of creed, may perhaps see it as significant that the *I Ching* was written at approximately the same time as the handing-down of the Ten Commandments and, discounting the likelihood of Judaism somehow influencing Chinese culture in the 87 short years after, could ascribe its writing to an alternative method used by God to get His message across to a different culture.

What thinking man today believes in a selective deity — one who would choose a single race alone to follow His teaching? The idea that a god would place upon the earth a host of different races, only for one of them to have an afterlife, is anathema. Reflection will show that all of the world's major religions have the same basic ground-rules. The differences are mainly cosmetic, designed to appeal to varying national temperaments.

It is more logical to believe that God would manifest Himself in different ways to different peoples at different times. It is therefore quite possible that the *I Ching* was God's method of instructing the Chinese. Today, whereas Christians and Jews read the Bible, and Moslems the Koran, the Chinese consult the *I Ching*. Perhaps the Westerner, with correct motivation and with faith in a universal spirit, may also obtain spiritual benefit from the study of the *I Ching*. Certainly, no harm can accrue from learning to improve one's behaviour towards one's fellow men and women.

THE FUNCTION OF THE *I CHING*

The *I Ching* encourages meditation by providing a greater awareness of the world and by teaching both self-knowledge and one's relationship to the world. It has been described as a comprehensive method of viewing the world and the universe as an organised whole. It creates order out of chaos. It also foretells the future. This latter idea is based upon the Chinese belief that the future develops in accordance with fixed laws and according to calculable numbers. If these numbers are known, future events can be calculated with absolute certainty. It does not, however, concern itself with frivolities such as the results of horse-races.

The *I Ching* has a personality of its own and must be approached with reverence in the manner of a student seeking instruction from a respected tutor. An open mind is essential, as is also the willingness to accept instruction. The *I Ching* is the result of the combined wisdom of the most respected Chinese sages, who lived thousands of years ago. It is therefore appropriate that its pronouncements should be treated with a certain respect. It must be remembered that the ancient authors of the book thought in a different way to us today, partly due to the then different structure of society and partly due to the underlying differences between Eastern and Western thought and education.

The answers obtained by consulting the *I Ching* may therefore sometimes appear to be obtuse. Reflection on an answer, however, will almost always provide proof of its appropriateness to the question. The *I Ching* is therefore an aid to meditation. One must first meditate upon the question and then upon the answer arrived at through the formation of the appropriate hexagram. The *I Ching* does not state that something is definitely going to happen; instead, it directs the questioner's attention to alternatives. The answers obtained show the probable consequences of one's actions if one chooses one path rather than another. This is the plain, basic function of the *I Ching*.

THE *NEW I CHING*

THE REASON BEHIND THE *NEW I CHING*

Until recently, the *I Ching* as we know it in the West, was the result both of Richard Wilhelm's definitive work and James Legge's brilliant translation in the nineteenth century. Legge's contribution, already mentioned, was a much clearer translation than any of his predecessors, but there were still obstacles in his translation to anyone wishing to comprehend the oracle. The greatest of these was that the reader, once he or she had formed a hexagram, had to look in ten different places for the components of the relevant answer.

In his edition of the Legge translation, in 1971, Raymond Van Over painstakingly combined many of Legge's appendices, resulting in the much less complex situation that the Judgement, Commentary, Symbolism and Lines, could all be found under the one heading, that of the relevant hexagram. Without Van Over's arrangement of the text, this new version would have taken many more years to prepare and would perhaps not have been as accurate as it is.

I first encountered the *I Ching* in 1983. I found it to be a most remarkable aid to decision-making. I had always regarded myself as a rather indecisive person, but as I found myself becoming more and more interested in the answers I obtained from the use of the *I Ching*, I found my indecisiveness disappearing. The book, where it didn't actually make decisions for me, helped me to make them for myself by pointing out the logic of different actions, together with the possible outcomes.

Like many people before me, however, I became somewhat disenchanted by the obscure symbolism of the text. The antics of princes, tigers and geese seemed to have no relevance to everyday modern life. Try as I might, I could find no more than a passing reference to the questions I asked. Initially, I tried to find fixed meanings for the key phrases that recur throughout the book, but unfortunately I failed to find any consistency. I realised that the phrases themselves drew their meanings from the context of the hexagrams in which they were used. There was therefore no short-cut to developing an overall understanding of the book. I was left with interpreting the prophecies as they occurred. I found this to be unsatisfactory, as I felt that accuracy was lost by the natural tendency to allow wishful thinking or personal fears to colour interpretations of the text.

I determined to undertake a thorough rewrite of the *I Ching*, into modern-day language and concepts. My task was not made any the easier by the necessity of not detracting in even the slightest measure from the original meaning of the text. Several modern versions I had encountered had fallen prey to this failing and I did not intend that mine would be the same. Neither did I intend to create my new version of the oracle only for it to contain my own ideas and concepts, rather than those of the original authors. As I progressed with my work, I became encouraged by each step I took. When I saw the new version taking shape, hexagram by hexagram, I was spurred on to complete the work. Where one word would suffice instead of three or four, I used it. The result was a clarified and simplified text. In particular, my translation of the Lines uses economy of words, encouraging the essential function of the text to act as a catalyst to the reader's intuition.

By way of example, the text of the Judgement in the Legge translation for Hexagram 48, CHING (A Well), is as follows:

> JUDGEMENT — Looking at Ching, we think of how the site of a town may be changed, while the fashion of its walls undergoes no change. The water of a well never disappears and never receives any great increase, and those who come and those who go, can draw and enjoy the benefit. If the drawing has nearly been accomplished, but, before the rope has quite reached the water, the bucket has broken, this is evil.

As may be seen from this book, under Hexagram 48, my version of the Judgement is as follows:

> JUDGEMENT — Ching represents mutual helpfulness, as

symbolised by the unchanging nature of a well, the value of which being dependent on the extraction of water from it.

The reader will see how much clearer is the second version. To start with, it is simpler and easier to understand and also it shows the meaning of the hexagram more plainly than does the first version. Reflection will show that none of the original meaning has been lost. My greatest difficulty came with translating the Lines. The original Lines, as composed by the Duke of Chou, sometimes strayed from the context of the hexagrams to which they related. My task was therefore to bring them within the context of their appropriate hexagrams, whilst at the same time leaving them basically unchanged from their original individual meanings. For an example, let us examine Hexagram 50, TING (The Cauldron). The text for the Line, 9 in the 2nd place, was in the original:

> *9 in the 2nd place.* The second line, undivided, shows the cauldron with the things to be cooked in it. If its subject can say "My enemy dislikes me, but he cannot approach me", there will be good fortune.

Under Hexagram 50, my version of the Line is as follows:

> *9 in the 2nd place.* Caution will give enemies nothing at which to point.

Again, the reader can see how much clearer is the second version. It is much simpler to understand; it doesn't waste words and the original meaning has not been lost. The text still requires meditation, but this is made easier by the simplified text.

HOW TO CONSULT THE *NEW I CHING*

In order to consult the *New I Ching*, one must first have a question in mind. The best type of question is a direct one such as, "Should I do such-and-such at this time?" or, "Will my meeting with so-and-so be successful tomorrow?" The best procedure is to write the question on a piece of paper, so that it is not forgotten. One is then ready to consult the oracle. A hexagram must be obtained, from which a reading may be taken that will hopefully go some way towards answering the question. To arrive at the relevant hexagram, the questioner must surrender to the laws of chance.

Traditionally, there are two ways of constructing a hexagram: by manipulating a quantity of yarrow-stalks, or by tossing three coins. The manipulation of yarrow-stalks may have a profoundly ritualistic effect, but most readers will prefer to take the simpler and infinitely less time-consuming step of tossing three coins. For this reason, the yarrow-stalk procedure will not be described.

The questioner should take three coins. The denomination of the coins is unimportant, although it is better that they be of the same denomination. Heads are usually used to represent Yang; tails, Yin. Each head thrown counts as 3, each tail, 2. There are four types of lines that can be formed by a throw of three coins, as shown in Figure 3.

FIGURE 3 — THE LINES

Coins show	*Score*	*Represented by*
3 TAILS	6 (moving line)	——x——
2 TAILS, 1 HEAD	7 (young Yang)	————
1 TAIL, 2 HEADS	8 (young Yin)	—— ——
3 HEADS	9 (moving line)	——o——

Figure 3: **Using three coins to obtain the lines of a hexagram**

The required hexagram is constructed by the process of throwing the three coins six times. They are thrown by placing them in cupped hands, shaking them and then dropping them. It is preferable to do this over the middle of a table, so that the coins do not roll off. The value of the coins (heads 3, tails 2) is added up and the corresponding line drawn on a piece of paper below the written question. The first line is used as the base of the hexagram and the subsequent lines are written above it. The hexagram is constructed from the bottom to the top and the process of throwing the three coins is repeated six times, until the hexagram has been formed. Consider the following example, shown in Figure 4.

FIGURE 4 — FORMING A HEXAGRAM

Step 1

Our first throw is 1 Tail and 2 Heads.
This scores 8. We write:

Step 2

Our second throw is 3 Heads.
This scores 9. We write:

Step 3

Our third throw is 1 Tail and 2 Heads.
This scores 8. We write:

Step 4

Our fourth throw is 1 Tail and 2 Heads.
This scores 8. We write:

Step 5

Our fifth throw is 2 Tails and 1 Head.
This scores 7. We write:

Step 6

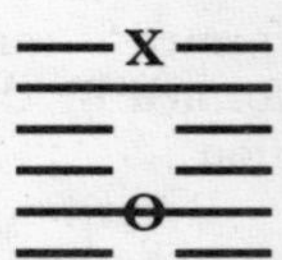

Our sixth throw is 3 Tails.
This scores 6. We write:

Figure 4. Example of forming a hexagram

We have now formed a Hexagram. Initially ignoring the moving nature of the lines, we have:

But we cannot ignore the moving lines. Moving lines derive their names from their nature, which is a tendency to reverse their polarity. Thus a moving 6 (—**X**—) whilst being initially a broken line, will change to a solid line (————). Similarly a moving 9 (——o——) will change from a solid line to a broken line (—— ——).

In the example shown in Figure 4, the hexagram formed will therefore change to an entirely different one, as shown in Figure 5.

FIGURE 5 — THE EFFECT OF MOVING LINES ON A HEXAGRAM

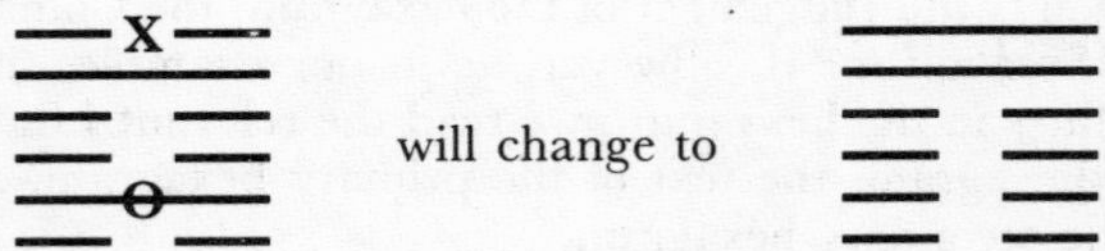

Figure 5. The effect of moving lines on a hexagram

The next step is to consult the key to the hexagrams, on page 29. The top row should be used to find the top trigram, and the side column, the bottom trigram. From the chart, find the number of the hexagram. In our example the first hexagram formed is number 29, K'AN (Perilous Pit). The hexagram then formed by the moving lines is number 20, KUAN (Contemplation).

Returning to the piece of paper on which the question has been written and under which the first hexagram has been constructed, write the new hexagram, formed by the moving lines, alongside the first one. Assume that the question is, "Should I change my job at this time?" The piece of paper will now look like Figure 6.

FIGURE 6 — PIECE OF PAPER ON WHICH QUESTION IS WRITTEN

Q. Should I change my job at this time?

29 — K'an (Perilous Pit)	20 — Kuan (Contemplation)

Figure 6. Example of a question and the resulting hexagrams

It is now time to obtain the readings. If there are no moving lines, and therefore no secondary hexagrams, we read only the text, which is the Judgement of the hexagram, the Commentary and the Symbolism. If, however, as in our example, there are moving lines in the hexagram, we read the relevant Lines of the primary hexagram, the text of the primary hexagram, and the text of the secondary hexagram.

Using our example, turn to Hexagram 29. Read the lines first, as in Figure 7.

FIGURE 7 — EXTRACT FROM HEXAGRAM 29

9 in the 2nd place	**Although danger is inescapable, it will not increase — and —**

6 at the top	Inability to get out of danger, even at its height, will lead to ill-fortune.
JUDGEMENT	K'an represents danger, and how to get out of it. Worthy action by the right-minded will be of high value.
COMMENTARY	K'an indicates the advisability of knowing when to act and when not to act in dealing with peril. Propriety and righteousness will prevail against the threat of danger.
SYMBOLISM	K'an symbolises the need to be always vigilant in the maintaining of virtues, so that danger can be dealt with whenever it may occur.

Figure 7. Extract from Hexagram 29

This provides the readings for the two moving lines and the text of the first, primary hexagram. Now turn to Hexagram 20 and read the text as in Figure 8.

FIGURE 8 — EXTRACT FROM HEXAGRAM 20

JUDGEMENT	Kuan represents the way we should appear to others — with sincerity and an appearance of dignity.
COMMENTARY	Kuan indicates how the superior should be looked up to by inferiors.
SYMBOLISM	Kuan symbolises the advisability of examining the needs of the people, prior to deciding policy.

Figure 8. Extract from Hexagram 20

This completes the readings, which must now be interpreted within the context of the question and in the light of our knowledge of the situation.

Quite frequently, hexagrams will be formed without any moving lines. More often than not, however, at least one moving line will be thrown and this will necessitate the forming of a new hexagram. The total number of readings, or permutations, that can be obtained with the hexagrams is 64^2, or 4096, which is considered to be sufficient to express all human conditions or situations.

It only remains for me to wish you success in your relationship with the *New I Ching*. As in all things, practice and perseverance will enhance and increase knowledge of the book and will open up a greater understanding of the wealth of advice in its pages. Through this can self-development be achieved.

KEY TO THE HEXAGRAMS

FIGURE 9

Upper Trigram → / Lower Trigram ↓	☰	☳	☵	☶	☷	☴	☲	☱
☰	1	34	5	26	11	9	14	43
☳	25	51	3	27	24	42	21	17
☵	6	40	29	4	7	59	64	47
☶	33	62	39	52	15	53	56	31
☷	12	16	8	23	2	20	35	45
☴	44	32	48	18	46	57	50	28
☲	13	55	63	22	36	37	30	49
☱	10	54	60	41	19	61	38	58

THE HEXAGRAMS

1

CH'IEN .... Creative

Upper Trigram Ch'ien ....heaven

Lower Trigram Ch'ien ....heaven

JUDGEMENT Ch'ien represents originality, correctness and advantageousness.

COMMENTARY Ch'ien indicates cause and effect. Dignity and wisdom is likewise indicated. Change and transformation are called for, to preserve harmony.

SYMBOLISM Ch'ien symbolises strength; also renewal and change, in the manner of the revolving of the heavens. The subject should adopt ceaseless activity.

LINES

9 in the 1st place
It is not the time for action.

9 in the 2nd place
It is time to appear and make oneself known.

9 in the 3rd place
The proper path must be trodden, day and night.

9 in the 4th place
There will be no error in advancing now.

9 in the 5th place
It is time to rouse oneself to one's work.

9 at the top
Remove complacency; adopt humility and modesty.

2

☷ **K'UN** .... Receptive

Upper Trigram	☷	K'un	earth
Lower Trigram	☷	K'un	earth

JUDGEMENT K'un represents originality, correctness and advantageousness, through subordination and docility. The subject should not take the initiative, but should follow. Others of like persuasion and principles should be sought to follow with the subject. Quietness will bring good fortune.

COMMENTARY Whereas Ch'ien originates, K'un gives birth to what has been originated. Where quietness is pursued, the effect will be great.

SYMBOLISM K'un symbolises the capacity and sustaining power of the earth.

LINES

6 in the 1st place
The ice is too thin; wait for it to thicken.

6 in the 2nd place
Straightness leads to advantageousness.

6 in the 3rd place
Excellence should be maintained, but hidden.

6 in the 4th place
Through carefulness, no blame or injury will occur.

6 in the 5th place
Correctness and humility will bring good fortune and honour.

6 at the top
Do not be too submissive, lest others take advantage of you.

3

CHUN .... Initial Difficulty

Upper Trigram 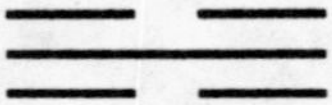 K'an .... water

Lower Trigram Chen .... thunder

JUDGEMENT Chun represents progress and success, after initial difficulties. Prudence and caution must be exercised prior to action. Advantage will come from unswerving correctness, and from delegating duties to the good and able.

COMMENTARY Chun indicates moving in perilousness, which requires skill and correctness. Delegation should not breed indifference.

SYMBOLISM Chun symbolises relief after oppression.

LINES

9 in the 1st place
Despite initial difficulty, perseverance and humility will finally triumph.

6 in the 2nd place
Although difficulties persist, steadfastness will bring success.

6 in the 3rd place
The subject holds fast, realising that unguided progress brings regret.

6 in the 4th place
On finding assistance, advance will be advantageous.

9 in the 5th place
Good fortune will not come from attempting great things now.

6 at the top
At the height of peril lies retreat and failure.

4

MENG ...... Youthful Inexperience

Upper Trigram	Ken	....	mountain
Lower Trigram	K'an	....	water

JUDGEMENT Meng represents youth and inexperience and the method of dealing with it by the experienced elder. The teacher does not seek the pupil; it is the pupil who seeks enlightenment. When the pupil opens his or her mind, the teacher fills it and there will be progress and success. But if the pupil does not listen, the teacher will cease to instruct.

COMMENTARY Meng indicates the good sense of seeking instruction where knowledge is lacking, and being receptive to that instruction.

SYMBOLISM Meng symbolises the passing of knowledge from the old to the growing. The subject should remember that, at no matter what the time of life, there is more growing to do; no matter how much has been learnt, there is still more to learn.

LINES

6 in the 1st place
Punishment is a short-term step only, for removing ignorance.

9 in the 2nd place
The good teacher exercises patience and humility, learning even from the most ignorant.

6 in the 3rd place
A person of youth and domestic inexperience should not be married.

6 in the 4th place
No good can arise from stubborn ignorance.

6 in the 5th place
Good fortune will come from the willingness to learn.

9 at the top
All do, or are done to, in accordance with their nature.

5

HSU .... Waiting

Upper Trigram K'an ....water

Lower Trigram Ch'ien ....heaven

JUDGEMENT Hsu represents the advisability of waiting until success is certain before undertaking hazardous enterprises. Through waiting will come success.

COMMENTARY Hsu indicates the advantageousness of subduing impetuosity.

SYMBOLISM Hsu symbolises the virtue of patience. The subject should be occupied in other pursuits, whilst waiting for the right time to come.

LINES

9 in the 1st place
Normal life should be led until the time is right.

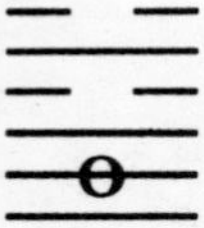

9 in the 2nd place
Precipitous action should not be occasioned by insults.

9 in the 3rd place
Unprepared and undefended advance will bring failure.

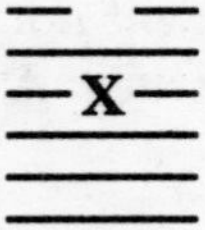

6 in the 4th place
In perilous situations, unpreparedness calls for retreat.

9 in the 5th place
Patience after triumph, brings further triumph.

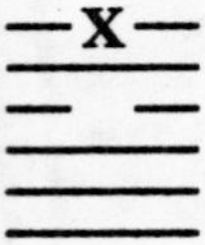

6 at the top
Unsolicited aid, gratefully received, will assure good fortune.

6

SUNG .... Conflict

Upper Trigram Ch'ien ....heaven

Lower Trigram K'an ....water

JUDGEMENT Sung represents opposition and strife. Through wariness will come good fortune. However, even wariness will not prevail against prolonged strife. A great enterprise would be rash.

COMMENTARY Sung indicates the advisability of changing course in the face of strife.

SYMBOLISM Sung symbolises opposition and contention. The subject should take advice before even entering into a strife-laden situation.

LINES

6 in the 1st place
In avoiding contention, derision may arise, but the end will be good.

9 in the 2nd place
When feeling unequal to a struggle, retreat is called for.

6 in the 3rd place
Remaining still, or advancing no more than is necessary, will bring good fortune.

9 in the 4th place
The realisation that it is right not to act, will lead to good fortune.

9 in the 5th place
Action now, will bring great fortune.

9 at the top
Persistence in strife will end in defeat.

7

SHIH .... Group Action

Upper Trigram K'un .... earth

Lower Trigram K'an .... water

JUDGEMENT Shih represents the presence of good fortune and lack of error, resulting from group action as ordered by the experienced person, provided that both the cause and action are right.

COMMENTARY Shih indicates the willingness of people to follow a trusted leader, even into ruin. Therefore the cause and effect must be right and proper.

SYMBOLISM Shih symbolises the good fortune that will arise from rightful action.

LINES

6 in the 1st place
A cause or action that is not right will lead to failure.

9 in the 2nd place
If confidence is placed in the leader, there will be good fortune.

6 in the 3rd place
Divided authority will lead to failure.

6 in the 4th place
In these prevailing circumstances, it is right to retreat.

6 in the 5th place
Only defensive actions are right; only sole leadership will succeed.

6 at the top
The incompetent should not be allowed to lead others.

8

PI .... Union

Upper Trigram K'an .... water

Lower Trigram K'un .... earth

JUDGEMENT Pi represents the concept of union between different classes and levels of people. The subject who would wish others to follow, should examine his or her own fitness to lead. If worthy, others will unite under the subject and good will come from it, but only if they do not delay.

COMMENTARY Pi indicates good fortune arising from inferiors uniting, to follow docilely their superior. But some do not wish for union until it is too late and ill-fortune occurs.

SYMBOLISM Pi symbolises the tendency to seek close and complete union.

LINES

6 in the 1st place
The seeking of union will bring other advantages.

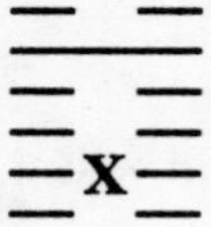

6 in the 2nd place
The desire for union stems from right thinking.

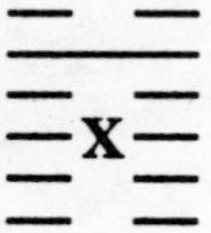

6 in the 3rd place
Union is sought with undesirable people and ill-fortune is indicated.

6 in the 4th place
Union is sought with the proper person; correctness will bring good fortune.

9 in the 5th place
The subject who originates union, inspires confidence and trust.

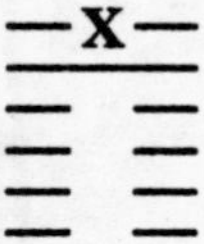

6 at the top
Seeking union when it is too late will lead to ill-fortune.

9

HSAIO CH'U .... Taming Force

Upper Trigram	Sun	............wood, wind
Lower Trigram	Ch'ien	.........heaven

JUDGEMENT Hsaio Ch'u represents restraint in small things, such action leading to progress and success.

COMMENTARY Hsaio Ch'u indicates that exercising restraint in small measures will bring success.

SYMBOLISM Hsaio Ch'u symbolises the ability temporarily to restrain. The subject should restrain the outward appearance of virtue.

9 in the 1st place
The strong-natured will continue advancing and there will be good fortune.

9 in the 2nd place
Adhering to duty will bring good fortune.

9 in the 3rd place
Through lack of restraint will come ill-fortune.

6 in the 4th place
Apprehension is misplaced in the restraint of others.

9 in the 5th place
The sincere person unites others in common cause.

9 at the top
Once achieved, restraint should be sustained or there will be ill-fortune.

10

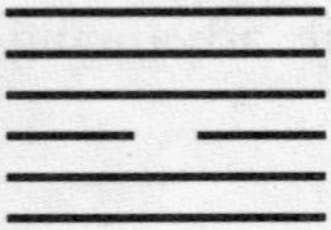

☰☱ (hexagram)

LU .... Treading Carefully

Upper Trigram ☰ Ch'ien ....heaven

Lower Trigram ☱ Tui ....marsh, lake

JUDGEMENT Lu represents success, brought about by treading carefully through life.

COMMENTARY Lu indicates weakness triumphing over strength, through caution.

SYMBOLISM Lu symbolises the advisability of being mindful of the proper place of different people in the nature of things.

9 in the 1st place
Being right-minded, to go forward sure-footed will lead to no error.

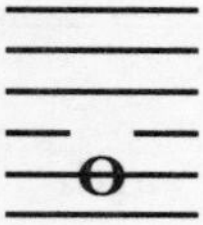

9 in the 2nd place
The quiet person takes the steady path and there will be good fortune.

6 in the 3rd place
To advance with more ability in mind than in fact will lead to disaster.

9 in the 4th place
Knowledge of peril will bring care in action and there will be good fortune.

9 in the 5th place
The higher one is exalted, the greater will one fall.

9 at the top
If every step has been right, the result will be good.

11

T'AI .... Peace

Upper Trigram ☷ K'un .... earth

Lower Trigram ☰ Ch'ien ....heaven

JUDGEMENT T'ai represents the growth of peace between opposing factors and the resultant good fortune.

COMMENTARY T'ai indicates the peaceful union of the strong with the weak. The subject should coexist with inferiors.

SYMBOLISM T'ai symbolises the arranging by the benefactor of gifts, so as to facilitate easy access to their benefits by the recipients.

LINES

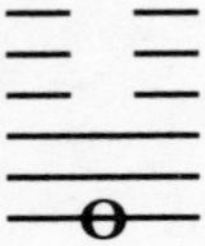

9 in the 1st place
Determined advance will bring good fortune.

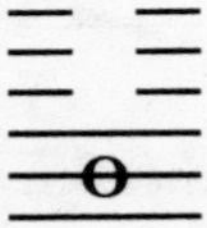

9 in the 2nd place
Through adaptation will come peaceful enjoyment of strength.

9 in the 3rd place
Realisation of the changing nature of things will bring peace.

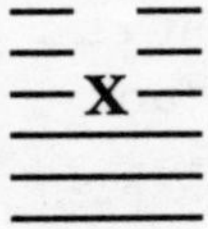

6 in the 4th place
Unsolicited aid will be given freely and willingly.

6 in the 5th place
Proper action will lead to great good fortune.

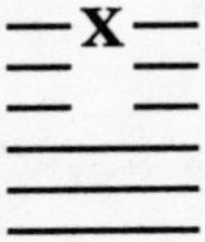

6 at the top
Long and sustained neglect of defence will bring defeat.

12

䷋ **P'I** .... Stagnation

Upper Trigram	☰	Ch'ien	heaven
Lower Trigram	☷	K'un	earth

JUDGEMENT P'i represents stagnation and decay after growth has finished. Lack of understanding between different classes of people will lead to ill-fortune.

COMMENTARY P'i indicates the necessity of rulers taking the initiatives.

SYMBOLISM P'i symbolises avoiding calamity by concealing virtues.

LINES

6 in the 1st place
Open-mindedness will encourage loyalty.

6 in the 2nd place
Patience and obedience will resolve problems fortunately.

6 in the 3rd place
Shame is felt even in the thought of wrong.

9 in the 4th place
Action that is ordained by heaven will be successful.

9 in the 5th place
Caution is needed, even in the midst of success.

9 at the top
Even the worst distress must change to good fortune.

13

䷌ **T'UNG JEN** .... Companionship

Upper Trigram ☰ Ch'ien ....heaven

Lower Trigram ☲ Li .... fire

JUDGEMENT T'ung Jen represents the virtue of unselfish union or companionship. The greatest difficulties will be dealt with, ending in progress and success. The subject should remember to act correctly at all times.

COMMENTARY T'ung Jen indicates intelligence supported by strength of character.

SYMBOLISM T'ung Jen symbolises the naturalness of desiring union.

LINES

9 in the 1st place
Even the desire for union must be conceived in unselfishness.

6 in the 2nd place
Union of like with like only, is narrow-minded and will lead to regret.

9 in the 3rd place
The weaker person long refrains from union with the stronger, avoiding misfortune.

9 in the 4th place
Caution and right-mindedness will lead to good fortune.

9 in the 5th place
The subject who desires union will conquer opposition and achieve their desire.

9 at the top
Although union is only partly achieved, there will be no ill-fortune.

14

TA YU .... Abundance

Upper Trigram Li .... fire

Lower Trigram Ch'ien ....heaven

JUDGEMENT Ta Yu represents a state of prosperity.

COMMENTARY Ta Yu indicates strength directed by intelligence and the benefits obtained by acting always at the proper time.

SYMBOLISM Ta Yu symbolises the properness of always distinguishing between good and evil.

LINES

9 in the 1st place
Acting correctly, whilst mindful of difficulties, will lead to no ill.

9 in the 2nd place
An abundance of virtues will bring no losses in the conducting of affairs.

9 in the 3rd place
The undeserving, lacking virtue, will assume airs.

9 in the 4th place
Restraint of power, occasions no-one injury.

6 in the 5th place
Sincerity concealed by majesty leads to good fortune.

9 at the top
Tempered strength will always bring good fortune.

15

CH'IEN .... Modesty

Upper Trigram K'un .... earth

Lower Trigram Ken .... mountain

JUDGEMENT Ch'ien represents the way to permanent success through modesty and humility.

COMMENTARY Ch'ien indicates the high value set upon humility. The subject should be humble and success will be achieved.

SYMBOLISM Ch'ien symbolises the virtue of dealing with everyone on their own level.

LINES

6 in the 1st place
People who humble themselves to the level of others will have good fortune.

6 in the 2nd place
Humility in action will bring good fortune.

9 in the 3rd place
Modesty in accomplishment will ensure sustained success.

6 in the 4th place
The successful and prosperous should maintain humility.

6 in the 5th place
The humble will find all their movements advantageous.

6 at the top
Humility will aid the recognition of limitations.

16

YU .... Harmony

Upper Trigram Chen .... thunder

Lower Trigram K'un .... earth

JUDGEMENT Yu represents a state of harmony and happy contentment.

COMMENTARY Yu indicates how contentment moves people to obedience.

SYMBOLISM Yu symbolises the joy felt after problems have been resolved.

LINES

6 in the 1st place
Drawing attention to one's own pleasure will bring cause for regret.

6 in the 2nd place
The upright person who also possesses foresight will gain good fortune.

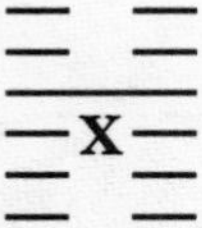

6 in the 3rd place
Idle hedonism will lead to no good.

9 in the 4th place
The subject who creates and maintains harmony will enjoy sustained success.

6 in the 5th place
Weakness allows pleasure to gain control, but will eventually subdue it.

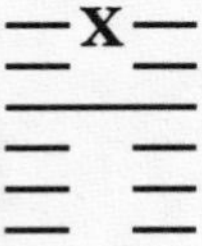

6 at the top
Even the weakest-willed will survive, if they will only change.

17

SUI .... Following

Upper Trigram — Tui ....marsh, lake

Lower Trigram — Chen ....thunder

JUDGEMENT Sui represents the idea of following. Where everything is proper, there will unmistakeably be great progress and success.

COMMENTARY Sui indicates holding in esteem those above one.

SYMBOLISM Sui symbolises how action is always followed by reaction.

LINES

9 in the 1st place
Unselfish and right-minded changing of course will bring merit.

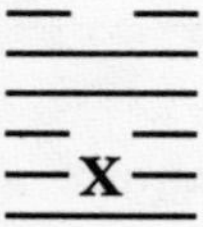

6 in the 2nd place
The following of inexperience leaves no room for the gaining of experience.

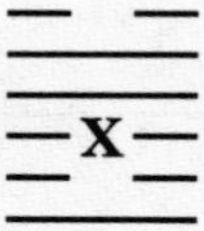

6 in the 3rd place
The subject who follows experience, rather than inexperience, will find what is sought.

9 in the 4th place
Only sincere loyalty will save from misfortune the subject who is followed.

9 in the 5th place
The true seeking of excellence will bring good fortune.

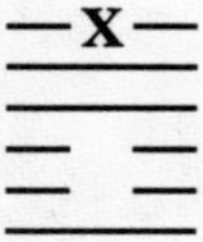

6 at the top
Only what is right must be followed.

18

☶☴ **KU** .... Arresting Decay

Upper Trigram ☶ Ken ....mountain

Lower Trigram ☴ Sun ....wood, wind

JUDGEMENT Ku represents the arresting of decay and restoration to soundness of a state of ruin. Great efforts will be required to achieve this, but great progress and success will result.

COMMENTARY Ku indicates the creation of order out of disorder.

SYMBOLISM Ku symbolises disorder. Helping people will be a saving virtue.

LINES

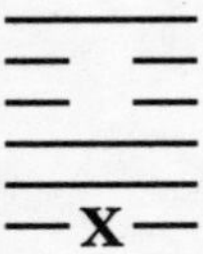

6 in the 1st place
Concealing the blame of others will lead to good fortune.

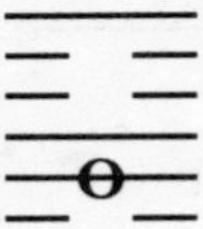

9 in the 2nd place
Gentle correction will lead to rightness.

9 in the 3rd place
Excesses countered by submission will bring no misfortune.

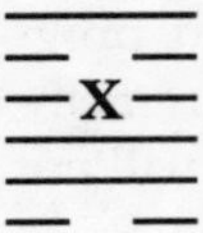

6 in the 4th place
Indulgence when going forward will lead to failure.

6 in the 5th place
Correct dealings will bring praise.

9 at the top
Non-participation on this occasion will provide correct example.

19

LIN .... Approach

Upper Trigram ☷ K'un ....earth

Lower Trigram ☱ Tui ....marsh, lake

JUDGEMENT Lin represents the approach of authority. Proper behaviour will be advantageous and there will be great progress and success. It is well to remember, though, that the authority will not always be present.

COMMENTARY Lin indicates strength, leading to pleasure and compliancy.

SYMBOLISM Lin symbolises the approaching by superiors to their inferiors, in order to secure their support.

LINES

9 in the 1st place
When the will is set on doing what is right, there will be good fortune.

9 in the 2nd place
Going forward now will be advantageous.

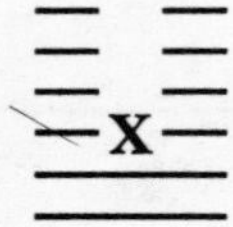

6 in the 3rd place
Willingness to go forward in these circumstances will lead to ill, but care will improve matters.

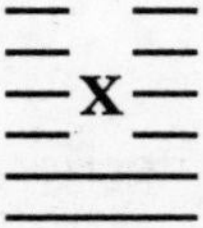

6 in the 4th place
Advancing with the highest intentions will lead to no ill.

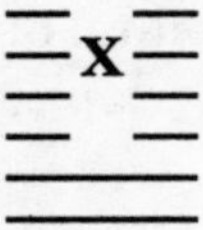

6 in the 5th place
Authority advancing with wisdom will bring good fortune.

6 at the top
Honesty and generosity will lead to good fortune.

20

䷓ **KUAN** .... Contemplation

Upper Trigram ☴ Sun ....wood, wind

Lower Trigram ☷ K'un .... earth

JUDGEMENT Kuan represents the way we should appear to others — with sincerity and an appearance of dignity.

COMMENTARY Kuan indicates how the superior should be looked up to by inferiors.

SYMBOLISM Kuan symbolises the advisability of examining the needs of the people, prior to deciding policy.

LINES

6 in the 1st place
Thoughtlessness and near-sightedness are inferior behaviour.

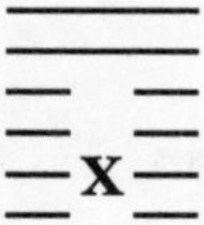

6 in the 2nd place
Reticence and timidity are reprehensible in a male.

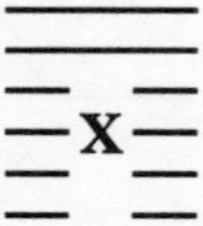

6 in the 3rd place
Docility will bring about action only at the proper time.

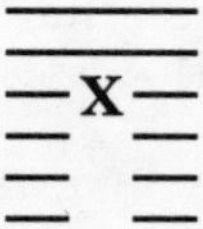

6 in the 4th place
Contemplation of the superiority of others will give birth to ambition.

9 in the 5th place
Self-examination and unselfish consideration will bring no ill.

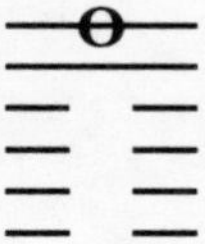

9 at the top
Contemplation of one's own character will lead to improvement.

21

SHIH HO .... Biting Through

Upper Trigram — Li .... fire

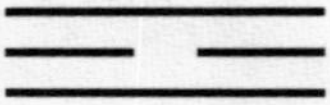

Lower Trigram — Chen .... thunder

JUDGEMENT Shih Ho represents the advantageousness of using legal constraints to remove obstacles to union, so that different levels may come together satisfactorily.

COMMENTARY Shih Ho indicates judgement tempered by leniency.

SYMBOLISM Shih Ho symbolises the union of majesty and intelligence, in the forming of judgements.

LINES

9 in the 1st place
The recipient of initial punishment may be deterred from repeating error.

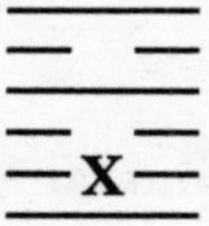

6 in the 2nd place
Effective action must be continued and increased, until the effect is achieved.

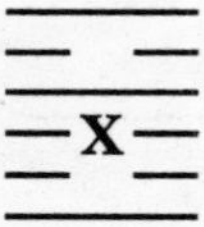

6 in the 3rd place
Applying punishment is disagreeable, but no great ill will occur.

9 in the 4th place
Strength with caution in adjudication will bring good fortune.

6 in the 5th place
Leniency in judgement will lead to no error.

9 at the top
The recidivist hears but does not listen; there will be ill-fortune.

22

PI .... Adornment

Upper Trigram — Ken .... mountain

Lower Trigram — Li .... fire

JUDGEMENT Pi represents adornment and ornamentation. It must be remembered, however, that adornment is secondary to substantiality.

COMMENTARY Pi indicates the necessity of ornament being kept in check by mindfulness of substantiality.

SYMBOLISM Pi symbolises appearances enhanced by adornment. In matters of truth, however, it must not be used.

LINES

9 in the 1st place
Ornamentation is not considered essential for rightful-living.

6 in the 2nd place
Ornamentation is ruled by substantiality.

9 in the 3rd place
Continual propriety will secure the respect of others.

6 in the 4th place
Substance is recognised as superior to ornament.

6 in the 5th place
Preference for simplicity and economy will bring good fortune.

9 at the top
The unornamented will achieve his or her aim.

23

PO .... Falling Apart

Upper Trigram Ken .... mountain

Lower Trigram K'un .... earth

JUDGEMENT Po represents the process of falling apart, or overthrowing. There is no advantage in any action.

COMMENTARY Po indicates the defeat of plans; such defeat, however, being regarded as just a transitory affair, as circumstances are certain to change for the better.

SYMBOLISM Po symbolises the strengthening of foundations, so as to secure the well-being and stability of the higher levels.

LINES

6 in the 1st place
Attempts to overthrow rightness will lead to evil.

6 in the 2nd place
Rightness overthrown will bring certain evil.

6 in the 3rd place
Correct motivation in overthrowing things will bring no ill.

6 in the 4th place
Imminent danger awaits he or she who has been overthrown.

6 in the 5th place
Motiveless advocation will lead to no blame.

9 at the top
Strength survives and gains fresh strength; there will be no more danger.

24

FU .... Returning

Upper Trigram K'un .... earth

Lower Trigram Chen .... thunder

JUDGEMENT Fu represents the idea of returning, or starting again. After decay has run its course, things can only improve and any movement will be advantageous.

COMMENTARY Fu indicates the naturalness of change and of rejuvenation.

SYMBOLISM Fu symbolises the return to rest after activity.

LINES

9 in the 1st place
To return, one must first have deviated from course; there will be great fortune.

6 in the 2nd place
Returning to the proper path is admirable and will lead to good fortune.

6 in the 3rd place
Repeated returns are perilous, but ill-fortune will be avoided by caution.

6 in the 4th place
Compromise will bring about a return to the proper path.

6 in the 5th place
Humble desire for self-improvement will lead to no ill.

6 at the top
Returning to an improper course will lead to disaster.

25

WU WANG .... Innocence

Upper Trigram Ch'ien .... heaven

Lower Trigram Chen .... thunder

JUDGEMENT Wu Wang represents sincere and unreckless simplicity. Recklessness will bring ill-fortune, but unswerving correctness will lead to great progress and success.

COMMENTARY Wu Wang indicates the blessed nature of innocence.

SYMBOLISM Wu Wang symbolises the correctness apparent in the nature of things.

LINES

9 in the 1st place
Sincere action will achieve what is desired.

6 in the 2nd place
Unselfish and good motivation will bring success.

6 in the 3rd place
Innocence will sometimes invite calamity.

9 in the 4th place
Adherence to correctness will occasion no ill.

9 in the 5th place
When ill befalls correctness, faith will affect a cure.

9 at the top
Completed actions should be followed by rest; more action would be calamitous.

26

TA CH'U .... Taming Force

Upper Trigram	Ken	mountain
Lower Trigram	Ch'ien	heaven

JUDGEMENT Ta Ch'u represents restraint and accumulation. In this way will things become stronger. Whomsoever intends to increase their virtue must be right-minded and the most difficult tasks will end in success.

COMMENTARY Ta Ch'u indicates a great accumulation of virtue, made stronger by the restraint of it. Correct motivation as a foundation will grow in strength to overcome the strongest opposition. No task will be too great to undertake.

SYMBOLISM Ta Ch'u symbolises the importance of experience and learning in the accumulation of virtue.

LINES

9 in the 1st place
To go forward now would lead to strong opposition.

9 in the 2nd place
Wisdom not to advance in the face of difficulties is blameless.

9 in the 3rd place
In the midst of peril, correctness will make advance in any direction advantageous.

6 in the 4th place
Precaution and anticipation will lead to great good fortune.

6 in the 5th place
Far-sighted precaution will obviate peril, and end in good fortune.

9 at the top
The way is free to accumulate virtue; there will be success.

27

I .... Nourishment

Upper Trigram Ken .... mountain

Lower Trigram Chen .... thunder

JUDGEMENT I represents the nourishing of body and mind. Right motivation is essential and there will be good fortune.

COMMENTARY I indicates the benefits obtained by nourishing talents and virtues for the greater good of all.

SYMBOLISM I symbolises the way that temperate eating nourishes the body and temperance in words nourishes the mind.

LINES

9 in the 1st place
Insubstantial effort will bring ill-fortune.

6 in the 2nd place
Seeking nourishment from improper sources will lead to evil.

6 in the 3rd place
Incorrect self-sufficiency will render any action disadvantageous.

6 in the 4th place
Seeking nourishment aids its giving; no error will occur.

6 in the 5th place
Even being able to depend on the strength of others, difficult tasks must not be undertaken.

9 at the top
The tasks of instruction and nourishment are hard, but there will be success.

28

TA KUO .... Excess

Upper Trigram — Tui ....marsh, lake

Lower Trigram — Sun ....wood, wind

JUDGEMENT Ta Kuo represents the extraordinary measures that are required in extraordinary times. These will bring success.

COMMENTARY Ta Kuo indicates that some situations call for flexibility in order that success may be achieved.

SYMBOLISM Ta Kuo symbolises extraordinary action and events.

LINES

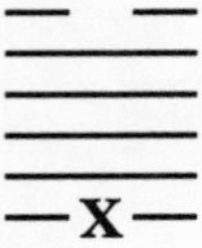

6 in the 1st place
Humility and carefulness will occasion no error.

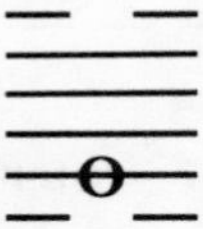

9 in the 2nd place
Extraordinary associations may still be fruitful.

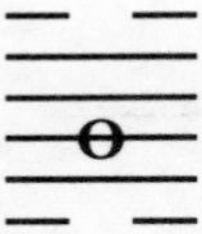

9 in the 3rd place
The extraordinary strain will be too great for one alone.

9 in the 4th place
There is strength enough; seeking aid will lead to regret.

9 in the 5th place
Fruitless associations will soon decay; there will be neither blame nor praise.

6 at the top
Attempts to do too much will lead to disaster, but no blame will accrue.

29

K'AN .... Perilous Pit

Upper Trigram K'an .... water

Lower Trigram K'an .... water

JUDGEMENT K'an represents danger and how to get out of it. Worthy action by the right-minded will be of high value.

COMMENTARY K'an indicates the advisability of knowing when to act and when not to act, in dealing with peril. Propriety and righteousness will prevail against the threat of danger.

SYMBOLISM K'an symbolises the need to be always vigilant in the maintaining of virtues, so that danger can be dealt with whenever it may occur.

LINES

6 in the 1st place
Any action now will only increase the danger.

9 in the 2nd place
Although danger is inescapable, it will not increase.

6 in the 3rd place
Unproductive movement will fail to extricate one from danger.

6 in the 4th place
When unable to avert danger, no ill will come from seeking aid.

9 in the 5th place
Danger is almost removed; there will be no error.

6 at the top
Inability to get out of danger, even at its height, will lead to ill-fortune.

30

☲☲ **LI** .... Brightness

Upper Trigram ☲ Li .... fire

Lower Trigram ☲ Li .... fire

JUDGEMENT Li represents brightness and intelligence. Humility attached to intelligence will bring good fortune.

COMMENTARY Li indicates the correctness of everything having its place. Docile acceptance of this fact will lead to success.

SYMBOLISM Li symbolises the cultivation of intelligence and the spreading of it.

LINES

9 in the 1st place
When the way is confused, carefulness will bring no error.

6 in the 2nd place
Adhering to the correct course will bring great good fortune.

9 in the 3rd place
Unnecessary discontentment will lead to evil.

9 in the 4th place
Abruptness is unbearable to others and will lead to disaster.

6 in the 5th place
Demonstrations of sorrow show inward humility; there will be good fortune.

9 at the top
Great achievements, if they contain humility, will occasion no error.

31

HSIEN .... Influence

Upper Trigram — Tui .... marsh, lake

Lower Trigram — Ken .... mountain

JUDGEMENT Hsien represents the exerting of influence; with correctness, it will lead to good fortune.

COMMENTARY Hsien indicates how correct influence may bring harmony and peace.

SYMBOLISM Hsien symbolises the keeping open of the mind in order that it be receptive to outside influences.

LINES

6 in the 1st place
Desire to influence is useless without the capability.

6 in the 2nd place
When unable to act unaided, it will be better to remain still.

9 in the 3rd place
Exercising influence now will lead to regret.

9 in the 4th place
Inadequacy calls for correctness, if there is to be good fortune.

9 in the 5th place
Unselfish influence in trivial matters will cause no regret.

6 at the top
Empty verbal influence will lead to no good.

32

䷟ **HENG** .... Perseverance

Upper Trigram ☳ Chen .... thunder

Lower Trigram ☴ Sun .... wood, wind

JUDGEMENT Heng represents perseverance in correctness, leading to progress and success.

COMMENTARY Heng indicates long continuance in the nature of things.

SYMBOLISM Heng symbolises unchanging activity and steadfastness.

LINES

6 in the 1st place
Premature desire for continuance will lead to evil.

9 in the 2nd place
Steadfastness will bring no cause for regret.

9 in the 3rd place
Non-continuity in the maintaining of virtue will cause regret.

9 in the 4th place
Continual fruitless searching will come to naught.

6 in the 5th place
Perseverance is correct in whatsoever is right.

6 at the top
Excessive perseverance will lead to evil.

33

TUN .... Retreat

Upper Trigram	Ch'ien	....	heaven
Lower Trigram	Ken	....	mountain

JUDGEMENT Tun represents the necessity of retreating before lesser people, when these have the majority. Correct behaviour will lessen the ill-effects of this action.

COMMENTARY Tun indicates that harmful circumstances can best be avoided by retiring.

SYMBOLISM Tun symbolises that even retreat is successful, in that harm fails to occur.

LINES

6 in the 1st place
Any movement would be disadvantageous; stillness will bring no disaster.

6 in the 2nd place
A firm purpose will not be broken.

9 in the 3rd place
People who would hinder retreat should be kept at a distance.

9 in the 4th place
Retreating, despite wishing not to, will bring good fortune.

9 in the 5th place
Retiring admirably and with correct purpose, will lead to good fortune.

9 at the top
Nobly retiring will be advantageous in every way.

34

TA CHUANG .... Great Power

Upper Trigram	Chen	thunder
Lower Trigram	Ch'ien	heaven

JUDGEMENT Ta Chuang represents the idea that rightness must govern strength and act in harmony with it in the conducting of all affairs.

COMMENTARY Ta Chuang indicates that great power must be exercised both impartially and unselfishly.

SYMBOLISM Ta Chuang symbolises strength being used to master self. The subject should be proper in every step taken.

LINES

9 in the 1st place
Advancing prematurely is exhausting and will certainly occasion distress.

9 in the 2nd place
Strength tempered by correctness will lead to good fortune.

9 in the 3rd place
Cautious use of strength will help avoid peril.

9 in the 4th place
Advancing with care and correctness will lead to good fortune.

6 in the 5th place
Strength controlled and directed will cause no regret.

6 at the top
Resting, due to awareness of weakness, brings good fortune.

35

䷢ **CHIN** .... Progress

Upper Trigram ☲ Li .... fire

Lower Trigram ☷ K'un .... earth

JUDGEMENT Chin represents progress, advance and improvement.

COMMENTARY Chin indicates advancing and the rewards obtained by so doing.

SYMBOLISM Chin symbolises the benefits obtained by striving to increase one's virtues.

LINES

6 in the 1st place
When virtue is unrecognised, it will be better to cease to advance.

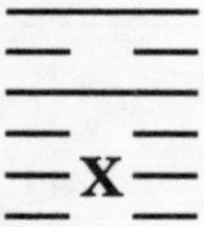

6 in the 2nd place
Persevering in advancing will bring good fortune.

6 in the 3rd place
The common aim is to advance; there will be no ill.

9 in the 4th place
Stealthy advance will lead to peril.

6 in the 5th place
Indifference as to the outcome will not affect any advance being advantageous.

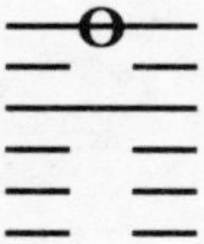

9 at the top
Although using force is regrettable, correctness will bring good fortune.

36

MING I .... Intelligence Wounded

Upper Trigram ☷ K'un .... earth

Lower Trigram ☲ Li .... fire

JUDGEMENT Ming I represents repression. It will be advantageous to recognise repression when it occurs and correctly maintain one's purpose.

COMMENTARY Ming I indicates the repression of what is good.

SYMBOLISM Ming I symbolises the virtue of concealing one's intelligence in the conducting of affairs.

LINES

9 in the 1st place
Halting one's advance, after an initial setback, may bring derision, but firm purpose must be maintained.

6 in the 2nd place
Impediment will not overcome duty and rightness; there will be good fortune.

9 in the 3rd place
Success will come, but patience must be exercised.

6 in the 4th place
Withdrawing from peril now will occasion little damage.

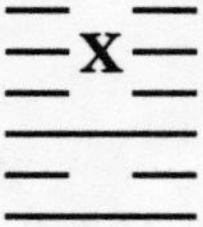

6 in the 5th place
Correctness will help avert total disaster.

6 at the top
Ingratitude will make for less of a person.

37

CHIA JEN .... Family

Upper Trigram	☴	Sun	...........wood, wind
Lower Trigram	☲	Li	.... fire

JUDGEMENT Chia Jen represents the regulation of the family, where each member plays his or her own part. The first thing necessary to its regulation is that the wife be correct in all things.

COMMENTARY Chia Jen indicates that, whereas authority must contain force, it must also be tempered by gentleness.

SYMBOLISM Chia Jen symbolises the virtue of consistency and correctness in regulating the family.

LINES

9 in the 1st place
Early rule-making will lessen later errors.

6 in the 2nd place
When a wife confines herself to her wifely duties, there will be good fortune.

9 in the 3rd place
Severity is better than laxity, if good fortune is desired.

6 in the 4th place
A family ruled by affection and harmony will have great fortune.

9 in the 5th place
The correctness of a man will be reflected in his family.

9 at the top
The good example of a man to his children will bring good fortune

38

K'UEI .... Disunion

Upper Trigram — Li .... fire

Lower Trigram — Tui .... marsh, lake

JUDGEMENT K'uei represents a state of division and how this condition can be corrected.

COMMENTARY K'uei indicates a state of being where separate wills do not move in the same direction.

SYMBOLISM K'uei symbolises the idea of disunion, even in the midst of general agreement.

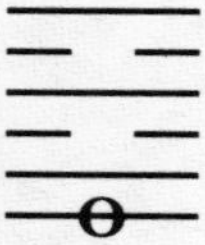

9 in the 1st place
Disappointment will occur unless common cause is found. Goodness may bring success.

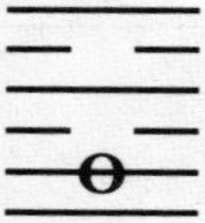

9 in the 2nd place
A chance meeting may lead to a better understanding.

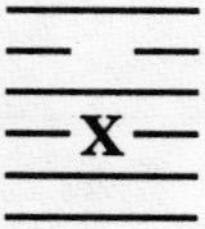

6 in the 3rd place
Whatever is bad now will eventually become good.

9 in the 4th place
Disunion giving way to union will bring success.

6 in the 5th place
Close and easy union will lead to success.

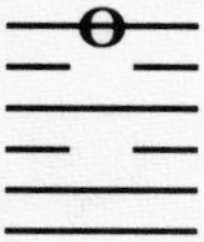

9 at the top
Discovering an enemy to be a friend will bring good fortune.

39

CHIEN .... Arresting Movement

Upper Trigram K'an .... water

Lower Trigram Ken .... mountain

JUDGEMENT Chien represents varying circumstances — some requiring action, others inaction. Irrespective of circumstances, correctness is needed at all times for there to be good fortune.

COMMENTARY Chien indicates prudent caution in the face of difficulty. When peril is in sight, it is best to cease to advance.

SYMBOLISM Chien symbolises the value of reflection and self-examination when faced with peril or uncertainty.

6 in the 1st place
Advancing now will increase difficulties; it will be better to await a more favourable time.

6 in the 2nd place
Although unable to cope with difficulties, correctness will bring no blame.

9 in the 3rd place
Unsupported advance will be difficult; it is best to wait for a better time.

6 in the 4th place
It is better to unite with one stronger and wait till the proper time.

9 in the 5th place
The greatest difficulties can be coped with; friends will give assistance.

6 at the top
There is nowhere to go; merit will come from remaining still.

40

CHIEH .... Removing Obstacles

Upper Trigram		Chen	thunder
Lower Trigram		K'an	water

JUDGEMENT Chieh represents removing obstacles and difficulties. When this is done, it is better not to change the old ways. Any action should be taken early and there will be good fortune.

COMMENTARY Chieh indicates the movement of peril, or removal of danger.

SYMBOLISM Chieh symbolises the raising of oppression. The subject should be gentle and merciful.

LINES

6 in the 1st place
The subject will commit no error.

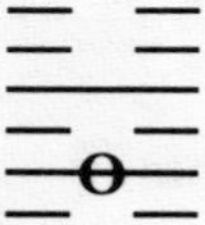

9 in the 2nd place
Straightforwardness and correctness will bring good fortune.

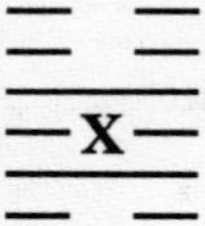

6 in the 3rd place
Obvious vulnerability invites attack; there will be cause for regret.

9 in the 4th place
Circumstances are unfavourable; no good will occur.

6 in the 5th place
The removal of all obstacles is accomplished; there will be good fortune.

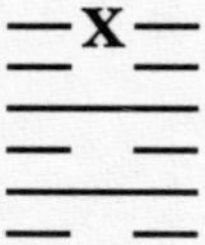

6 at the top
Correct aims will lead to advantageous effect.

41

SUN .... Decrease

Upper Trigram ☶ Ken .... mountain

Lower Trigram ☱ Tui .... marsh, lake

JUDGEMENT Sun represents diminishing or decrease. Willing decrease of assets, such as the correct payment of taxes, will bring great good fortune and advantage.

COMMENTARY Sun indicates the regulating of contributions according to means. No matter how small the contribution, if it be given willingly and sincerely, there will be advantage.

SYMBOLISM Sun symbolises that whatever decreases one, increases another.

LINES

9 in the 1st place
In desiring to help others, one's own affairs should not be neglected.

9 in the 2nd place
Action will lead to ill; inaction will be of greater assistance.

6 in the 3rd place
Many repetitions of thoughts or actions will cause doubts; single-mindedness will bring success.

6 in the 4th place
Difficulties will be lessened by seeking aid; there will be no regret.

6 in the 5th place
Humbly welcoming assistance will lead to great good fortune.

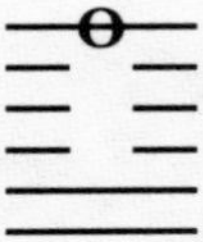

9 at the top
Giving to others, without diminishing one's own resources, will bring good fortune and advantage.

42

I .... Increase

Upper Trigram Sun ....wood, wind

Lower Trigram Chen .... thunder

JUDGEMENT I represents addition, or increase. Movement in any way will lead to advantage.

COMMENTARY I indicates unrestricted increase and the pleasure attained by it.

SYMBOLISM I symbolises the increasing of what is good and the diminishing of what is bad.

LINES

9 in the 1st place
Early movement is rash, but great success will bring no blame.

6 in the 2nd place
Assets are increased by gifts; correctness will bring good fortune.

6 in the 3rd place
Adversity will bring out the good from even the most evil.

6 in the 4th place
Unselfish advance will be acceptable and there will be advantage.

9 in the 5th place
Everyone benefits from the truly good person; there will certainly be great good fortune.

9 at the top
Selfish concern for increase will lead to great peril from others.

43

KUAI .... Removing Corruption

Upper Trigram — Tui .... marsh, lake

Lower Trigram — Ch'ien ....heaven

JUDGEMENT Kuai represents the way of dealing with wrong-doers. The subject who would undertake this task must denounce the wrong-doer and inspire the support of others. This should be done as peaceably as possible and there will be advantage in every way.

COMMENTARY Kuai indicates that there must be no selfish motive in the removal of wrong-doers.

SYMBOLISM Kuai symbolises that whatever is accumulated must subsequently be redispersed, as clouds which form from evaporation afterwards turn to rain.

LINES

9 in the 1st place
Precipitous and unprepared advance will lead to failure.

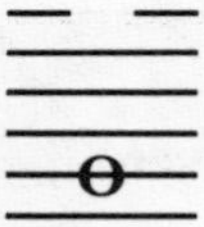

9 in the 2nd place
Righteous determination, tempered by caution, will protect from harm.

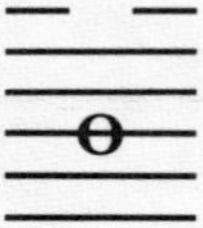

9 in the 3rd place
Irresolute appearance may annoy others, but no blame will be incurred.

9 in the 4th place
Solitary action is useless; failure to listen to advice to follow others will lead to no good.

9 in the 5th place
Strength of character will be needed to overcome bad influence, even in mind.

6 at the top
There is no-one to ask for help; misfortune will occur.

44

KOU .... Encountering

Upper Trigram	☰	Ch'ien ....heaven
Lower Trigram	☴	Sun ....wood, wind

JUDGEMENT Kou represents suddenly encountering, or casually meeting.

COMMENTARY Kou indicates the unexpected encountering of shameless boldness.

SYMBOLISM Kou symbolises the act of penetrating everywhere.

6 in the 1st place
Correct restraint against evil, in both body and mind, will lead to good fortune.

9 in the 2nd place
Dealing with evil oneself, to protect others, will bring no error.

9 in the 3rd place
There is peril, but no corruption has occurred; there will be no ill.

9 in the 4th place
Standing alone, impatient and lacking forebearance, will lead to evil.

9 in the 5th place
Patience and restraint until the proper time will render subsequent actions effective.

9 at the top
Restricting one's action to non-communication with evil will cause regret, but no blame.

45

TS'UI .... Gathering Together

Upper Trigram — Tui .... marsh, lake

Lower Trigram — K'un .... earth

JUDGEMENT Ts'ui represents collecting, or gathering together. Correctness in so doing will bring success and advantage in every movement.

COMMENTARY Ts'ui indicates the natural tendency of things to unite together.

SYMBOLISM Ts'ui symbolises the necessity of protecting a union from being dispersed.

LINES

6 in the 1st place
When unable to achieve union oneself, seeking aid will lead to success.

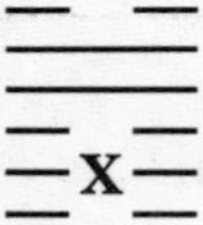

6 in the 2nd place
Being aided and encouraged by one stronger will bring good fortune.

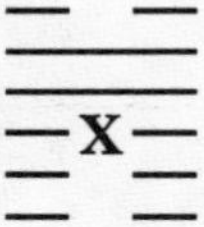

6 in the 3rd place
Despite difficulties, desire for union will be successful, although some small regret will occur.

9 in the 4th place
Caution is needed for there to be success and no blame.

9 in the 5th place
Union has been achieved, but correctness and dignity will be needed for there to be no error.

6 at the top
Unable alone to achieve union, the desire for it will occasion no error or blame.

46

SHENG .... Ascending

Upper Trigram K'un .... earth

Lower Trigram Sun ....wood, wind

JUDGEMENT Sheng represents advancing upwards, or ascending. Force with modesty will bring great progress and success.

COMMENTARY Sheng indicates gradual growth, leading to fulfilment.

SYMBOLISM Sheng symbolises the desirability of careful attention to one's virtue and the nurturing of it until it has grown to maturity.

LINES

6 in the 1st place
Humility and docility will lead to advance upwards being welcomed.

9 in the 2nd place
Sincerity and devoted loyalty will lead to no error.

9 in the 3rd place
Bold and fearless advance upwards is presumptuous.

6 in the 4th place
Worthiness is recognised; there will be good fortune.

6 in the 5th place
Correctness will lead to easy advance and good fortune.

6 at the top
When all has been achieved, further advance will be blind and fruitless.

47

K'UN .... Oppression

Upper Trigram Tui .... marsh, lake

Lower Trigram K'an ....water

JUDGEMENT K'un represents oppression, or repression of good by bad. Great correctness is required for there to be good fortune and no error.

COMMENTARY K'un indicates strength obscured by weakness. The subject needs to be correct, for the oppression to be lifted.

SYMBOLISM K'un symbolises a condition of distress.

LINES

6 in the 1st place
Extreme stupidity will lead to distress being increased.

9 in the 2nd place
During oppression, action will lead to evil, although no blame will be incurred.

6 in the 3rd place
Reckless action will lead to success.

9 in the 4th place
The slowness of giving help to others will cause regret, but the outcome will be good.

9 in the 5th place
Sincerity and docility will facilitate the overcoming of distress.

6 at the top
At the height of distress, repentance will bring good fortune.

48

CHING .... A Well

Upper Trigram K'an ....water

Lower Trigram Sun ....wood, wind

JUDGEMENT Ching represents mutual helpfulness, as symbolised by the unchanging nature of a well, the value of which being dependent on the extraction of water from it.

COMMENTARY Ching indicates that the bucket must reach the water and be drawn to the top unbroken for there to be any benefit.

SYMBOLISM Ching symbolises the stimulation of others to mutual helpfulness.

LINES

6 in the 1st place
Corrupt and useless men will be held in low regard.

9 in the 2nd place
Lack of cooperation from others will lead to failure.

9 in the 3rd place
Assistance that is available but not taken will benefit no-one.

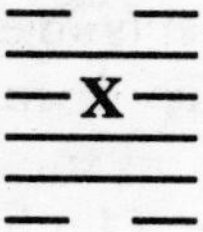

6 in the 4th place
Self-absorbtion will benefit no others; neither blame nor praise will occur.

9 in the 5th place
Everyone draws upon what is available; fulfilment will occur.

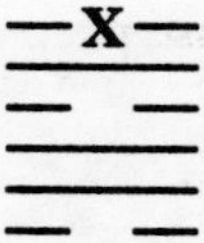

6 at the top
Inexhaustible and general availability of benefits will lead to great good fortune.

49

KO .... Revolution

Upper Trigram	Tui	....	marsh, lake
Lower Trigram	Li	....	fire

JUDGEMENT Ko represents the nature of necessary change. Change is viewed with suspicion and dislike, until its effects are manifested; only then is it believed in and accepted. Great progress and success will arise from the change, if both its motivation and result be good and correct.

COMMENTARY Ko indicates that people's dislike of change is overcome only in retrospect.

SYMBOLISM Ko symbolises the need to choose properly the time for change.

9 in the 1st place
Change made too early will render any action impossible.

6 in the 2nd place
Action taken now to change will have fortunate results.

9 in the 3rd place
Reckless and violent change would be perilous; only with caution and due deliberation will the end be good.

9 in the 4th place
If the confidence of others is secured, action and change will be advantageous.

9 in the 5th place
Change is believed in by others; action will be advantageous.

6 at the top
Correctness lies in taking no solitary action; there will be good fortune.

50

TING .... The Cauldron

Upper Trigram Li .... fire

Lower Trigram Sun ....wood, wind

JUDGEMENT Ting represents the nourishing of talents and virtue, leading to great progress and success.

COMMENTARY Ting indicates how people of great worth should be nourished.

SYMBOLISM Ting symbolises the need for total correctness, for perfection to be achieved.

LINES

6 in the 1st place
Advantage will come from getting rid of what is bad; there will be no error.

9 in the 2nd place
Caution will give enemies nothing at which to point.

9 in the 3rd place
There is now failure, but correctness will bring good fortune in the end.

9 in the 4th place
Being unequal to the task, and unaided, will result in evil.

6 in the 5th place
Correctness will bring about advantage.

9 at the top
All has been accomplished; there will be great good fortune and any action will be advantageous.

51

CHEN .... Exciting Power

Upper Trigram Chen .... thunder

Lower Trigram Chen .... thunder

JUDGEMENT Chen represents the conduct that should be pursued in times of exciting power, or movement, by the person most interested in the situation. Through care and precaution will any peril be averted.

COMMENTARY Chen indicates ease and development.

SYMBOLISM Chen symbolises the necessity of cultivating one's virtues and examining one's faults.

LINES

9 in the 1st place
When the correct time comes, apprehension will prove unfounded; there will be good fortune.

6 in the 2nd place
In times of peril, one should try to extricate oneself; things will eventually return to the way they were before.

6 in the 3rd place
When distraught, action and movement will lead to no mistake.

9 in the 4th place
There is nothing to do; things will only get worse.

6 in the 5th place
Risk is always present, but safety will come in the end.

6 at the top
Action will lead to evil, but precaution will reduce the effect to that of censure.

52

KEN .... Arresting Movement

Upper Trigram ☶ Ken .... mountain

Lower Trigram ☶ Ken .... mountain

JUDGEMENT Ken represents resting or stopping; resting in what is right, or stopping by arresting movement.

COMMENTARY Ken indicates resting when it is time to rest and acting when it is time to act. From this will come advantage. There should be no consciousness of self in one's resting or moving.

SYMBOLISM Ken symbolises the need to confine one's actions to those of one's position in life.

6 in the 1st place
From the first, only what is right should be done; there will be no error and caution will lead to advantage.

6 in the 2nd place
Dissatisfaction will come from being unable to help others.

9 in the 3rd place
There is peril; disorder and anger will occur.

6 in the 4th place
Self alone can be kept from agitation; there will be no error.

6 in the 5th place
Lack of rashness in speech will remove any occasion for repentance.

9 at the top
Restfulness, generosity and goodness will lead to good fortune.

53

CHIEN .... Gradual Progress

Upper Trigram Sun ....wood, wind

Lower Trigram Ken .... mountain

JUDGEMENT Chien represents gradual progress or growth. Correctness will lead to advantage.

COMMENTARY Chien indicates gradual progress, as in the marriage of a young woman, where each step is properly carried out from its initiation to its consummation.

SYMBOLISM Chien symbolises how extraordinary virtue may be achieved and maintained by the gradual nature of its growth.

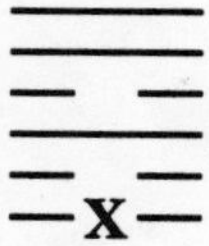

6 in the 1st place
Danger exists through circumstances, not self; there will be no error.

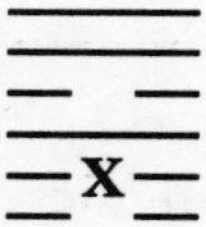

6 in the 2nd place
Ease and fulfilment, if earned, will lead to good fortune.

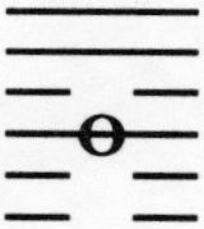

9 in the 3rd place
Strength, though failing in duty, will be useful in the end.

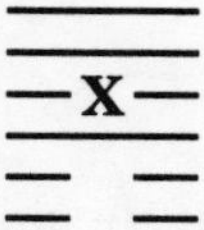

6 in the 4th place
Humility and right will overcome shortcomings; there will be no error.

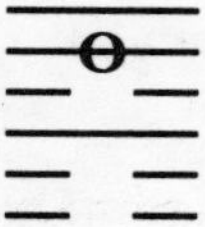

9 in the 5th place
Though being a victim of circumstances, in the end there will be good fortune.

9 at the top
After all is done, other usefulness will lead to good fortune.

54

KUEI MEI .... Propriety

Upper Trigram Chen .... thunder

Lower Trigram Tui .... marsh, lake

JUDGEMENT Kuei Mei represents propriety and the way that breaches of propriety will lead to evil.

COMMENTARY Kuei Mei indicates the care that should be taken to ensure that propriety is maintained from the beginning, so that ill-fortune will not occur in the end.

SYMBOLISM Kuei Mei symbolises the way that small lapses of propriety may lead to larger evils.

LINES

9 in the 1st place
Despite apparent shortcomings, good service will lead to good fortune.

9 in the 2nd place
Faithful devotion will compensate for other deficiencies; there will be advantage.

6 in the 3rd place
Meanness and impropriety will lead to loss of position.

9 in the 4th place
Proper delay will lead to an improved result.

6 in the 5th place
Placing oneself second to another will lead to good fortune.

6 at the top
When proprieties are not observed, the effect will be failure and no advantage.

55

FENG .... Prosperity

Upper Trigram Chen .... thunder

Lower Trigram Li .... fire

JUDGEMENT Feng represents abundance and prosperity, in which condition lack of anxiety will lead to progress and development.

COMMENTARY Feng indicates the nature of prosperity. It is the nature of all things to change; as such, prosperity will change to poverty. It is wise to try to maintain prosperity for as long as possible.

SYMBOLISM Feng symbolises the necessity of correctness and exactness in all judgements.

9 in the 1st place
Prosperity will be maintained by mutual helpfulness.

6 in the 2nd place
Advice to others will be treated with suspicion; sincerity is needed for there to be good fortune.

9 in the 3rd place
Great things should not be attempted, but correctness will lead to no error.

9 in the 4th place
Even in darkness, meeting of like with like will lead to good fortune.

6 in the 5th place
If aided by others, the result will be admirable and there will be good fortune.

6 at the top
Selfish solitariness will occasion ostracism; no-one will help and there will be evil.

56

LU .... Travelling Stranger

Upper Trigram Li .... fire

Lower Trigram Ken .... mountain

JUDGEMENT Lu represents the process of travelling and how those so doing should conduct themselves. Through humility and integrity will harm be averted and attainment and progress achieved.

COMMENTARY Lu indicates the qualities needed in a traveller to be restfulness, humility and intelligence.

SYMBOLISM Lu symbolises the exerting of wisdom and caution in all judgements.

LINES

6 in the 1st place
Selfishness and meanness will incur calamity.

6 in the 2nd place
When equipped with everything required, there will be no cause for complaint.

9 in the 3rd place
Arrogance and violence towards inferiors will place one in peril.

9 in the 4th place
Despite protection against peril, caution will give rise to apprehension.

6 in the 5th place
Good qualities will bring praise from others.

9 at the top
Arrogant behaviour and deafness to what is right will lead to evil.

57

SUN .... Gentle Penetration

Upper Trigram ☴ Sun ....wood, wind

Lower Trigram ☴ Sun ....wood, wind

JUDGEMENT Sun represents the process of gently correcting and improving. From this will come attainment and progress in small degrees, leading to advantage in any direction.

COMMENTARY Sun indicates the relationship between superiors and inferiors, in the way that rightful orders are given and obeyed, when their purpose is to remedy what is wrong.

SYMBOLISM Sun symbolises the agreement of people to orders that are right and just.

LINES

6 in the 1st place
In perplexity lies the need for firm command by others.

9 in the 2nd place
Sincerity of purpose will overcome distractions, leading to good fortune.

9 in the 3rd place
Restlessness and violence will be ineffective, and will lead to regret.

6 in the 4th place
All has been achieved, leading to success.

9 in the 5th place
Docility and correctness will bring good fortune.

9 at the top
Loss of justness will make any attempt at correctness result in evil.

58

TUI .... Joy, Pleasure

Upper Trigram	Tui	.... marsh, lake
Lower Trigram	Tui	.... marsh, lake

JUDGEMENT Tui represents pleasure or satisfaction. Correctness is essential for there to be progress and attainment.

COMMENTARY Tui indicates pleased satisfaction. This condition induces people to endure hard work and danger fearlessly.

SYMBOLISM Tui symbolises the virtue of encouraging friendship and union.

9 in the 1st place
Nothing has yet been done upon which to judge; inward harmony will lead to good fortune.

9 in the 2nd place
There will never be any wrongful action; sincerity will bring good fortune.

6 in the 3rd place
Excessive and selfish hedonism will lead to evil.

9 in the 4th place
Reflection and deliberation, before yielding to pleasure, will bring joy.

9 in the 5th place
Trusting in he or she who would injure one will lead to peril.

6 at the top
There is pleasure in attracting and leading others; correctness must be achieved in the treatment of pleasure.

59

HUAN .... Dispersion

Upper Trigram — **Sun** ....wood, wind

Lower Trigram — **K'an** ....water

JUDGEMENT Huan represents dispersion or dissipation. In men or women, this takes the form of alienation from what is right and good. Sincere religion is needed to remedy this fault. Hazardous enterprises can then be undertaken, provided that correctness and right are present.

COMMENTARY Huan indicates the progress and success that will be attained by maintaining firm correctness in what is right.

SYMBOLISM Huan symbolises the necessity of religion to the conquest of alienation from right and goodness.

LINES

6 in the 1st place
Weakness will need aid to deal with evil, even when it has not made much progress. There will be good fortune.

9 in the 2nd place
Seeking union will give shelter from evil.

6 in the 3rd place
Fearless selflessness will occasion no need for repentance.

6 in the 4th place
Dispersion, followed by the collection of the best elements, will bring great good fortune.

9 in the 5th place
As perspiration flows from the body, so will rightful orders flow from goodness.

9 at the top
Dissociation from peril will lead to no blame.

60

CHIEH .... Regulation

Upper Trigram K'an ....water

Lower Trigram Tui .... marsh, lake

JUDGEMENT Chieh represents regulating, or restraining. Regular divisions, if they fit in with circumstances and are not too severe, will lead to permanent success and attainment.

COMMENTARY Chieh indicates the impermanency of too severe rules, in that they cannot be maintained.

SYMBOLISM Chieh symbolises that excess in restraint will bring about the cessation of tolerance by those restrained.

LINES

9 in the 1st place
Lacking rashness and remaining still will occasion no error.

9 in the 2nd place
Remaining still when it is time to act will lead to evil.

6 in the 3rd place
Realisation that failure to obey rules leads to blame, will come too late. There will be sorrow.

6 in the 4th place
Quiet and natural deference to authority will lead to progress and success.

9 in the 5th place
Willing enactment of rules will bring good fortune.

6 at the top
Overly severe rulers will lead to repentance, but the situation will improve.

61

CHUNG FU ..... Inmost Sincerity

Upper Trigram — Sun .... wood, wind

Lower Trigram — Tui .... marsh, lake

JUDGEMENT Chung Fu represents the high quality of inmost sincerity. Lack of preoccupation and selfishness will lead to advantage.

COMMENTARY Chung Fu indicates the power of sincerity to bring about a happy state of cooperation between different levels of people.

SYMBOLISM Chung Fu symbolises the ability of sincerity to penetrate even the deepest questions or problems.

LINES

9 in the 1st place
Friendly sincerity in self alone will bring good fortune.

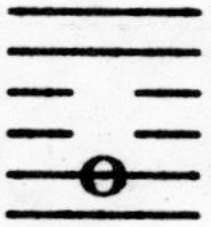

9 in the 2nd place
Deep love of sincerity will unite men in common cause.

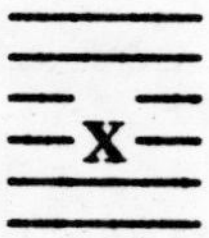

6 in the 3rd place
Sincerity not kept to self will suffer outside influence; there will be confusion.

6 in the 4th place
Discarding distracting influences will lead to greater sincerity.

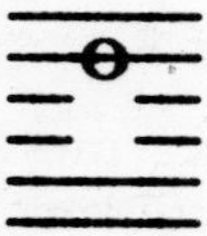

9 in the 5th place
Sincerity, bringing about close union with others, will bring no error.

9 at the top
Ineffectual movements, no matter how correct, will lead to harm.

62

䷽

HSAIO KUO ...... Small Excesses

Upper Trigram	☳	Chen	thunder
Lower Trigram	☶	Ken	mountain

JUDGEMENT Hsaio Kuo represents the permissability of small excesses in matters which are not essential to correctness and right.

COMMENTARY Hsaio Kuo indicates that small excesses may be carried out in small affairs and there will be good fortune.

SYMBOLISM Hsaio Kuo symbolises the correctness of exceeding in humility and economy.

LINES

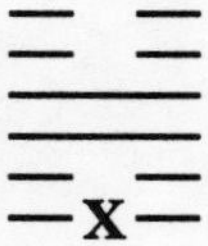

6 in the 1st place
Excessive lack of humility will unavoidably lead to evil.

6 in the 2nd place
Humble and loyal advance will occasion no error.

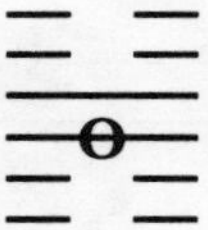

9 in the 3rd place
Overconfidence and lack of defensive measures will invite harm and lead to evil.

9 in the 4th place
Going forward will be perilous; the situation can be met without excessive action.

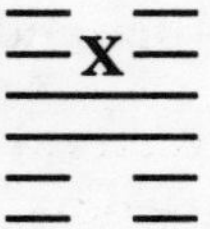

6 in the 5th place
There is peril, but no harm will occur.

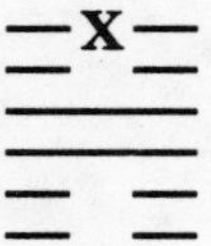

6 at the top
In not meeting the situation by exceeding the proper course, will come evil.

63

CHI CHI .... Completion

Upper Trigram  K'an .... water

Lower Trigram 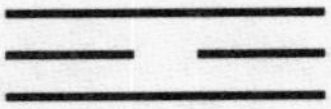 Li .... fire

JUDGEMENT Chi Chi represents completion, or successful accomplishment. Correctness is needed to obviate the natural instability of affairs, or what has been fortunate will turn to disorder.

COMMENTARY Chi Chi indicates the nature of change; order changes to disorder and disorder to order.

SYMBOLISM Chi Chi symbolises the need to anticipate evil and take precautions against it.

9 in the 1st place
After accomplishment should come rest; there will be no error.

6 in the 2nd place
Action is now improper; what is lost will eventually be found, when it is the time to act.

9 in the 3rd place
Long and tedious actions, despite their successful outcome, will lead to weariness.

6 in the 4th place
Caution is needed; precaution against evil will be wise.

9 in the 5th place
Patience and caution, with sincerity, will bring great good fortune.

6 at the top
Violent action at this time will lead to peril.

64

WEI CHI ...... Before Completion

Upper Trigram	Li	fire
Lower Trigram	K'an	water

JUDGEMENT Wei Chi represents a time prior to completion, before what is desired has been accomplished. Being mindful of the nature of change, it denotes, alternatively, a time when order has turned to disorder and the struggle to achieve order has recommenced.

COMMENTARY Wei Chi indicates that lack of caution in attempting to remedy disorder will lead to failure. With caution will come progress and success.

SYMBOLISM Wei Chi symbolises lack of harmony and order.

LINES

6 in the 1st place
Ignorant attempts at action will give cause for regret.

9 in the 2nd place
Correctness and restraint will lead to good fortune.

6 in the 3rd place
Going forward, despite the situation still not being remedied, will lead to evil.

9 in the 4th place
Correct and vigorous efforts to remedy disorder will gain encouragement and lead to good fortune.

6 in the 5th place
Sincerity and humility will lead to good fortune.

9 at the top
Confidence and quiet enjoyment of success will cause no error; overaction will lead to ill-fortune.

CONSULTING THE *I CHING*

Figure 3 (from page 23) and Figure 9 (from page 29) are repeated here for easy reference when consulting the oracle. Refer to page 23 for instructions on how to consult the *I Ching*.

FIGURE 3 — THE LINES

Coins show	*Score*	*Represented by*
3 TAILS	6 (moving line)	—x—
2 TAILS, 1 HEAD	7 (young Yang)	———
1 TAIL, 2 HEADS	8 (young Yin)	— —
3 HEADS	9 (moving line)	—o—

Figure 3. Using three coins to obtain the lines of a hexagram

KEY TO THE HEXAGRAMS

FIGURE 9

Upper Trigram → Lower Trigram ↓	☰	☳	☵	☶	☷	☴	☲	☱
☰	1	34	5	26	11	9	14	43
☳	25	51	3	27	24	42	21	17
☵	6	40	29	4	7	59	64	47
☶	33	62	39	52	15	53	56	31
☷	12	16	8	23	2	20	35	45
☴	44	32	48	18	46	57	50	28
☲	13	55	63	22	36	37	30	49
☱	10	54	60	41	19	61	38	58